United States Department of Agriculture

San Juan Bay Estuary Watershed Urban Forest Inventory

Thomas J. Brandeis, Francisco J. Escobedo, Christina L. Staudhammer, David J. Nowak, and Wayne C. Zipperer

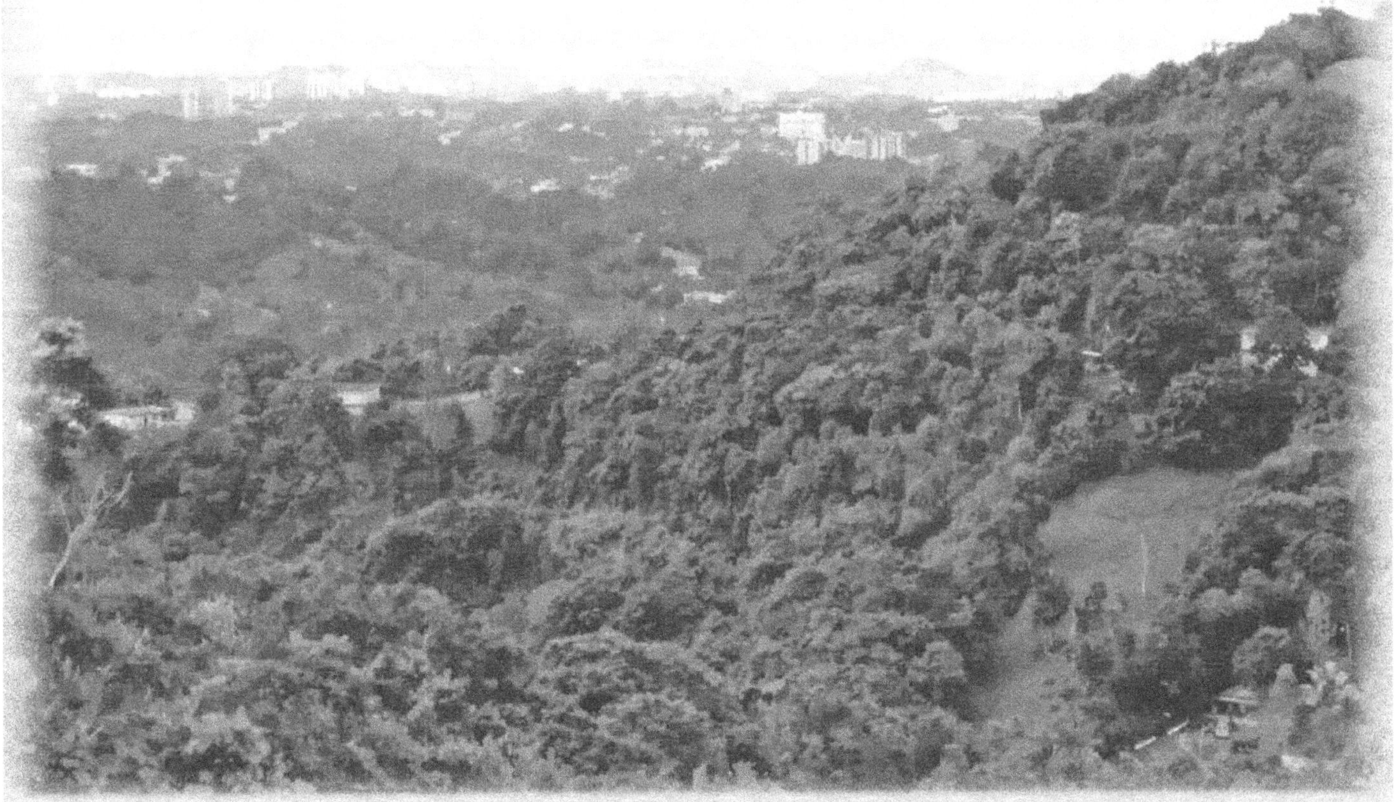

Forest Service   Southern Research Station   General Technical Report SRS-190

About the Authors

Thomas J. Brandeis is a Research Forester with the Forest Inventory and Analysis Research Work Unit, Southern Research Station, U.S. Forest Service, Knoxville, TN 37919.

Francisco J. Escobedo is an Associate Professor and State Extension Specialist at the School of Forest Resources and Conservation, University of Florida, Gainesville, FL 32611-0410.

Christina L. Staudhammer is an Associate Professor in the Department of Biological Sciences, University of Alabama, Tuscaloosa, AL 35487.

David J. Nowak is a Research Forester with the Effects of Urban Forests and their Management on Human Health and Environmental Quality Research Work Unit, Northern Research Station, U.S. Forest Service, Syracuse, NY 13210.

Wayne C. Zipperer is a Research Forester with the Integrating Human and Natural Systems in Urban and Urbanizing Environments Research Work Unit, Southern Research Station, U.S. Forest Service, Gainesville, FL 32611-0806.

All photos by Tom Brandeis, Southern Research Station, unless otherwise noted.

Cover photo: The southern portion of the San Juan Bay Estuary watershed, a hilly area with soils derived from volcanic materials, is less densely-developed and has higher tree cover. Note the limestone "mogote" hills rising from the coastal plain in the distance to the north.

March 2014
Southern Research Station
200 W.T. Weaver Blvd.
Asheville, NC 28804

www.srs.fs.usda.gov

San Juan Bay Estuary Watershed Urban Forest Inventory

Thomas J. Brandeis, Francisco J. Escobedo, Christina L. Staudhammer, David J. Nowak, and Wayne C. Zipperer

Structurally diverse, species rich patches of secondary subtropical forest are found throughout the San Juan metropolitan area.

Foreword

This report presents information on the forests, urban tree cover, and land use within the watershed of Puerto Rico's San Juan Bay Estuary (SJBE) as described by two urban forest inventories undertaken from 2001 to 2002 and 2010 to 2011. These urban forest inventories were integrated with the island-wide forest inventories of Puerto Rico that were carried out concurrently.

Forest inventories of all States, Commonwealths, Territories, and possessions of the United States are mandated by the Agricultural and Research Extension and Education Reform Act of 1998 (Farm Bill). These surveys are part of a continuing nationwide undertaking by the U.S. Forest Service (USFS) through its regional research stations. Southern Research Station (SRS) Forest Inventory and Analysis (FIA)—operating from its headquarters in Knoxville, TN, and offices in Asheville, NC, and Starkville, MS—is responsible for surveying the 13 Southern States (Alabama, Arkansas, Florida, Georgia, Kentucky, Louisiana, Mississippi, North Carolina, Oklahoma, South Carolina, Tennessee, Texas, and Virginia), the Commonwealth of Puerto Rico, and the Territory of the U.S. Virgin Islands. The USFS FIA program for Puerto Rico and the U.S. Virgin Islands is jointly funded and conducted by USFS, SRS, FIA, and the USFS International Institute of Tropical Forestry (IITF). The primary goal of these surveys is to develop and maintain the resource information needed to formulate sound forest policies and programs. Additional information about annual surveys is available at http://fia.fs.fed.us/.

The research project was a collaborative effort between the USFS, University of Florida School of Forest Resources and Conservation, and University of Alabama School of Biological Sciences. In addition to the SRS FIA program's involvement, two other USFS research units participated in this work: the Northern Research Station's Effects of Urban Forests and their Management on Human Health and Environmental Quality Research Unit, and the SRS' Integrating Human and Natural Systems Research Unit.

The mission of the first-mentioned research unit is to quantify the effects of urban forests and their management on human health and environmental quality. Scientists and technical staff collect and analyze various field measurements and develop computer programs to better understand the structure, functions, and benefits of urban forests across the world. Numerous user-friendly tools are also being developed to aid local constituents in analyzing the structure, functions, health, and value of their own urban forest resources. The Integrating Human and Natural Systems Research Unit seeks to improve the understanding of how people living in urban and urbanizing landscapes both influence and are influenced by natural environments. The unit's technology transfer centers aim to develop and communicate guidelines, models, and tools for natural resource professionals, policymakers, planners, and citizens.

This urban forest inventory report characterizes forest cover and structure in the SJBE watershed and quantifies some of the ecosystem services this forest delivers. We also describe ground cover within the watershed, list tree and shrub species found there, and examine forest health in terms of pests, diseases, and tree crown conditions for different land uses. Finally, we discuss the forest's current conditions, compare them to similar forests outside the watershed, and stress the importance of continued monitoring to provide decisionmakers and land managers with timely, useful information.

Additional information about any aspect of this survey may be obtained from:

Forest Inventory and Analysis Research Work Unit
U.S. Department of Agriculture Forest Service
Southern Research Station
4700 Old Kingston Pike
Knoxville, TN 37919
Telephone: 865-862-2000

Acknowledgments

We thank Robin Morgan and Terry Hoffman of the U.S. Department of Agriculture Forest Service's State and Private Forestry program for providing funding for the 2002 urban forest inventory. We also acknowledge funding of the 2010 data collection under the grant "Spatial distribution of invasive horticultural woody plants in urban landscapes" Tropical and Subtropical Agricultural Research (TSTAR-C FY2008), Humfredo Marcano and Luis Ortíz of SRS FIA for their assistance with data collection, Angie Rowe of SRS FIA for her work with training, Olga Ramos and Eileen Helmer of the IITF for compiling of geographic information system datasets, Iván Vícens of the IITF for assistance with data collection, Jeffrey Glogiewicz of Consultores Ambiental and the Fundación Puertorriqueña de Conservación for collecting field data in 2001–02, and Jeffrey Glogiewicz and Edgardo González with Centro para la Conservación del Paisaje for data collection in 2010–11. We would also like to thank the reviewers for comments and suggestions on the draft publication. We appreciate the cooperation of other public agencies and private landowners in providing access to measurement plots.

Iván Vícens, U.S. Forest Service International Institute of Tropical Forestry; Luis Ortíz, U.S. Forest Service Southern Research Station; Edgardo González, Centro para la Conservación del Paisaje; Humfredo Marcano, U.S. Forest Service Southern Research Station; Jeffrey Glogiewicz, Centro para la Conservación del Paisaje; and Francisco Escobedo, University of Florida.

Contents

San Juan Bay Estuary Watershed Urban Forest Inventory

Thomas J. Brandeis, Francisco J. Escobedo, Christina L. Staudhammer,
David J. Nowak, and Wayne C. Zipperer

Abstract

We present information on the urban forests and land uses within the watershed of Puerto Rico's 21 658-ha San Juan Bay Estuary (SJBE) based on urban forest inventories undertaken in 2001 and 2011. We found 2548 ha of mangrove and subtropical moist secondary forests covering 11.8 percent of the total watershed area in 2011. Average tree cover in the study area was 24.1 percent overall, ranging from 12.2 percent cover on commercial/industrial/transportation land uses to 69.0 percent on the watershed's mangrove forests. This forest cover was created by approximately 10.1 million trees, which stored 319 737 metric tons of carbon (C) in 2011 and sequester C at a rate of 28 384 metric tons/year. The estimated value of the C storage by trees in the SJBE watershed was $8.1 million with an annual C sequestration value of $718,113 in 2011, up from the 2001 values of $4.0 million in stored C and an annual rate of $349,261.

In 2011 approximately 19 000 megawatts of energy required for cooling buildings were avoided due to tree shading and climate effects in residential and commercial areas and equated to 1986 metric tons of avoided C emissions due to building energy effects.

The inventories identified 75 tree and shrub species in 2001 and 86 species in 2011. Red, black, and white mangroves (*Rhizophora mangle*, *Avicennia germinans*, and *Laguncularia racemosa*) were the most common species due to the watershed's extensive mangrove forests, while tulipán africano (*Spathodea campanulata*) and María (*Calophyllum antillanum*) were predominant species in the moist forest patches and developed land uses. The occurrence of tree pests, diseases, and natural or anthropogenic damage was relatively low (12.7 percent) and generally of minor severity. Tree crowns did not show appreciable amounts of dieback or defoliation.

Urban forest benefits can be increased by tree-establishment and protection programs as an estimated 16.8 percent of the estuary is potentially plantable. Benefits also can be lost by deforestation of the existing forest canopy caused by urban development and other activities. Proper planning and management can sustain or enhance the existing urban forest to increase the environmental and societal benefits from trees in the SJBE watershed.

Keywords: Caribbean, ecosystem services, FIA, forest inventory, Puerto Rico, subtropical forest, urban forest.

Introduction

The 21 658-ha San Juan Bay Estuary (SJBE) watershed lies along the northeast coast of the island of Puerto Rico. It is at the heart of the dynamic, expanding San Juan metropolitan area, which has a total population of 2,478,905 people according to the 2010 U.S. Census; the population density averages 3,215 persons/km^2 but in some areas exceeds 8,300 people/km^2 (Villanueva and others 2000). This ecologically important area encompasses San Juan Bay, several large lagoons and channels, and extensive wetlands and forests, all in close proximity to this densely populated area.

Historically, forest covered much of the estuary's watershed. Mangrove forest (composed of *Rhizophora mangle*, *Avicennia germinans*, and *Laguncularia racemosa*) fringed the bays and lagoons, where it was protected from the surf and wind. A diverse mix of species (*Casearia guianensis*, *Calophyllum antillanum*, *Coccoloba uvifera*, *Manilkara bidentata*, *Sideroxylon foetidissimum*, and *Tabebuia heterophylla*, to name just a few of the principal species) that grew in the moist coastal plain forests and scattered karst hills (known locally as mogotes) was found farther inland (Departamento de Recursos Naturales y Ambientales 2007, Little and Wadsworth 1989, Wadsworth 1950).

A subtropical moist forest remnant in the San Juan Bay Estuary watershed.

Today, however, forest cover in the estuary has been greatly reduced by human activities. The native Taíno peoples had little impact on the forests of the estuary (Domínguez Cristóbal 1989), but since the founding of San Juan by Juan Ponce de León in 1521, the estuary has been subjected to a long and continued decrease in forest cover, filling in of mangrove swamps, wetlands draining, stream channelization, and other hydrological modifications (Seguinot Barbosa 1996). Historical records and previous island-wide forest inventories have shown a pattern of deforestation for agricultural production, then abandonment of the agricultural land as manufacturing began to dominate the Puerto Rican economy, and finally reversion of the land to secondary forest (Birdsey and Weaver 1982, Franco and others 1997). This pattern of land use change also occurred in the SJBE watershed. Currently, near San Juan and other urban areas of Puerto Rico, former agricultural land and the remaining forest are now cleared for urban development (Grau and others 2008, López and others 2001, Martinuzzi and others 2007, Parés-Ramos and others 2008, Ramos González 2001, Thompson and others 2007).

The estuary's remaining forest cover is now greatly reduced, highly fragmented, and threatened by further urban development. Mangroves have been removed from the margins of many waterways, with losses ranging from 28 to 67 percent from 1936 to 1995 (U.S. Environmental Protection Agency 2007). But mangrove areas are generally not suitable for most types of urban development, so a large, relatively contiguous mangrove forest still exists within the estuary. This mangrove forest, the largest in Puerto Rico, is to some extent protected within the Piñones Commonwealth Forest (Villanueva and others 2000). Conversely, virtually none of the original moist coastal forest remains. Most of the estuary's land that formerly held moist coastal forest has been cleared due to its suitability for urban development. Small stands of secondary forest consisting of a mix of native and introduced species remain scattered in a matrix of urban development, particularly on the mogotes across the metropolitan area.

The reduction of forest cover in the SJBE watershed has wide-ranging consequences for both terrestrial and marine wildlife and human residents. Ten of the 160 species of birds, 4 of the 19 species of amphibians and reptiles, and the manatee (*Trichechus manatus*) that reside in the SJBE watershed are listed as threatened or endangered at a Federal or Commonwealth level (Villanueva and others 2000). The estuary and its wildlife provide recreational opportunities for San Juan residents. Activities in the estuary's lagoons and canals include picnicking, swimming, boating, fishing for tarpon (*Megalops atlanticus*) and snook (*Centropomus undecimalis*), crabbing, and shellfish collection. Recognizing the estuary's importance and the seriousness of the threats that this ecosystem faces, the U.S. Environmental Protection Agency added the SJBE to its National Estuary Program in 1992. The Río Piedras subwatershed within the larger SJBE was designated an Urban Long Term Research Area (ULTRA) by the National Science Foundation and Forest Service, U.S. Department of Agriculture (USFS) in 2010.

The presence of trees and green areas improves the quality of life for all San Juan residents (Seguinot Barbosa 1996).

Street trees in a residential neighborhood in San Juan, Puerto Rico.

San Juan's urban trees also have important aesthetic, psychological, and environmental value in this heavily urbanized environment. Street trees, gardens, green areas, and urban parks complement the architecture of a city and increase the economic value of properties. People form strong emotional and spiritual associations with trees, and their presence helps reduce stress for urban dwellers (Nowak and others 1997a). Additional evidence indicates that exposure to trees contributes positively to human health (Donovan and others 2013).

While some aspects of the importance of urban tree cover are difficult to express in concrete terms, trees also provide ecosystem services whose benefits can be valued monetarily to more clearly quantify their importance to planners and policymakers (see Jones and others 2013 for a review of the economic benefits of urban trees and Escobedo and others 2011 for a review of urban forest ecosystem services and disservices related to pollution mitigation). Dollar values can be placed on the benefits provided by urban trees in sequestering carbon (C), moderating temperature, improving air quality, and mitigating hydrological problems brought on by development. Trees in the urban forest can affect building energy use and can sequester C as they grow, contributing to an area's larger C balance (McPherson 1998, Nowak 1993, Nowak and Crane 2002, Rowntree and Nowak 1991). The blocking of solar radiation by tree canopies is particularly important in the tropical climate of San Juan. A single shade tree can block 70 to 90 percent of the solar radiation that would otherwise shine on a single-story home (Heisler 1986a, 1986b). Shade trees have the potential to reduce interior temperatures of adjacent, non-air-conditioned buildings, and provide significant energy savings to homes with air conditioning (Donovan and Butry 2009, Simpson and McPherson 1998).

On a larger scale, the cumulative effect of solar energy interception by tree canopies (shading buildings, cement, and asphalt surfaces) and their subsequent transpiration has the potential to counteract the urban "heat island" effect (Heisler and others 1995, McPherson 1994). Trees also facilitate the removal and mitigation of many air pollutants commonly emitted in urban areas. Some airborne pollutants are directly absorbed by tree leaf tissues, while other pollutants, especially particulates, are also physically filtered from the air as it passes through tree crowns (Abdollahi and Ning 1996; Nowak 1994, 2002; Nowak and others 1997b, 2006). Pollutants are eventually washed or blown off the tree, absorbed in the leaves, or deposited onto the forest floor, where chemical processes or the biologically active soil community can potentially break them down. Urban forests also can mitigate the effects of heavy precipitation. The prevalence of impervious surfaces in urban areas exacerbates problems with stormwater as tropical depressions and hurricanes can yield high levels of precipitation in a short time. Interception and evaporation of rainwater by trees, and infiltration through the permeable forest floor, can substantially reduce runoff and flooding (Armson and others 2013, McPherson and Rowntree 1991, Nowak and others 1997a).

Management to maximize the delivery of beneficial services, particularly in an area as biologically and ecologically diverse as the SJBE watershed, requires accurate assessments of current ecosystem conditions. The study's overall goal is to provide some of the necessary information to make such assessments. Specifically, we estimate how much of the watershed is covered with forest and trees; how many trees are in the urban forest; how much C is stored in those trees; what the average ground, tree, and shrub covers are for each developed land use; what the species composition of both forested land and planted trees is in urbanized areas; and how healthy those trees are in terms of pests, diseases, and tree crown conditions. Additionally, we examine how some of these factors have changed between 2001 and 2011.

Methods

Study Site

The SJBE watershed, bound north to south by 18°28' N and 18°19' N latitude and west to east by 66°90' W and 65°53' W longitude, falls within the subtropical moist forest life zone (sensu Holdridge 1967) (fig. 1). Mean annual rainfall is between 1500 and 1700 mm, with an average annual temperature measured at the Old San Juan Climate Station of 27.2 °C to 23.9 °C, with an annual average of 25.9 °C (Lugo and others 2011). The upper reaches of the SJBE watershed lie on the northern foothills of the Puerto Rican Cordillera Central. These volcanic rock-derived hills slope down to meet the coastal plains upon which lies the San Juan metropolitan area. The coastal plains are made of surficial deposits of alluvial materials, sands, and other components over sedimentary bedrock. The plains are punctuated in areas by steep-sided limestone mogote outcroppings. Detailed description of the substrates underlying the SJBE watershed can be found in Lugo and others (2011).

The southern portion of the San Juan Bay Estuary watershed, a hilly area with soils derived from volcanic materials is less densely developed and has higher tree cover. Note the limestone "mogote" hills rising from the Coastal Plain in the distance to the north.

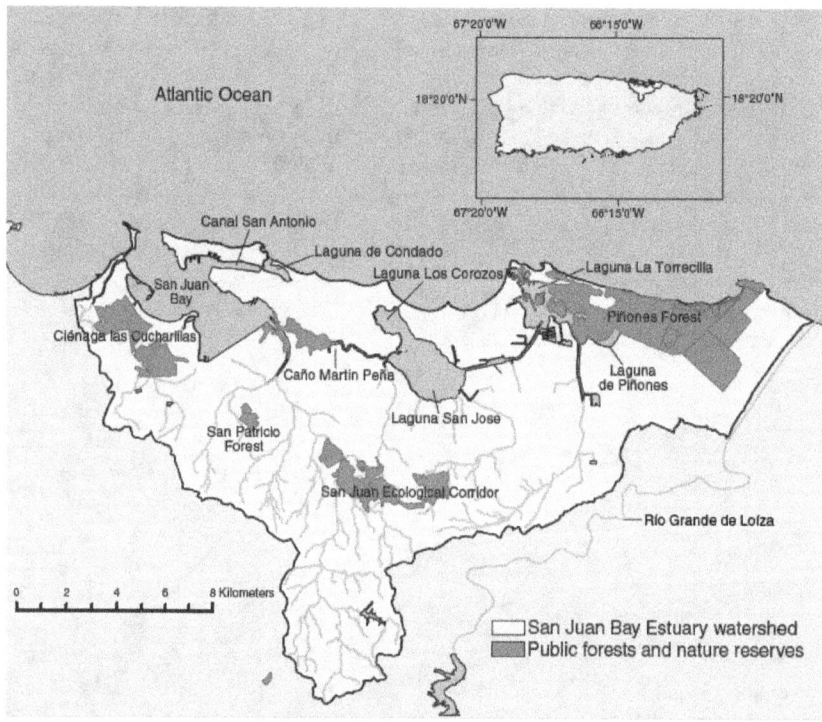

Figure 1—San Juan Bay Estuary's watershed in Puerto Rico.

4

The geomorphology and hydrology of the area are naturally complex and have been modified by human activities. The Río Bayamon lies along the western edge of the watershed and the Río Loíza along the west. The Río Piedras, Río Puerto Nuevo, and numerous smaller streams and channels also bring freshwater from the mountains into the watershed, where it mixes with saltwater from the Atlantic Ocean in the many estuarine areas such as San Juan Bay, Condado, San José Lagoon, La Torrecilla and Piñones Lagoons, and the channels that connect them. Dredging, landfills, and other human activities have changed the hydrological characteristics of the estuary considerably (Lugo and others 2011, Villanueva and others 2000).

Laguna San Jose in the San Juan Bay Estuary watershed, 2001. (photo by Jeffery Glogiewicz, Consultores Ambiental and the Fundación Puertorriqueña de Conservación)

Although most of the land in the SJBE watershed is privately owned, there are public forests and nature reserves, too. The 630-ha Piñones Commonwealth Forest falls entirely within the SJBE watershed to the northeast. The San Juan Ecological Corridor, a series of connected green spaces that includes the University of Puerto Rico's Experimental Station and Botanical Garden, and the Bosque Nuevo Milenio Urban Commonwealth Forest, has a total area of approximately 200 ha. Additionally, there is the small Bosque San Patricio Urban Commonwealth Forest (approximately 27 ha) on mogote hills within the watershed. The Ciénega las Cucharillas is an extensive saltwater and freshwater wetlands area in the northeastern portion of the watershed.

Mangrove forest in the Piñones Commonwealth Forest, Puerto Rico.

5

Urban Forest Inventory Sampling Design

Because we lacked a current land use map of the watershed to use for stratification, we chose to systematically sample the watershed. This approach will allow us to better follow long-term changes in land use in this highly dynamic landscape and to fully incorporate the urban forest inventory data into the concurrent island-wide forest inventory carried out by the USFS' Forest Inventory and Analysis (FIA) program (see Brandeis 2003, Brandeis and Turner 2013, Brandeis and others 2007 for details on the island-wide forest inventories).

The island-wide forest inventory provided a framework for our systematic sampling grid. The FIA program overlays a hexagonal sampling grid over the area to be inventoried (McCollum 2001, Reams and others 2005). Each hexagon in the standard FIA grid used on the continental United States has an area of approximately 2400 ha with a sampling plot in the center of each hexagon, or located a random distance and azimuth from that center (Reams and others 2005). Studies in North American cities indicated that two hundred 0.004-ha ($^1/_{10}$-acre) plots (for a total of 8.08 ha or 20 acres sampled) produced standard errors of 10 percent for estimates of the mean number of trees/ha over the entire urban area.[1] Broken down by land uses in the urban area, data from these studies yielded standard errors of 5.9 percent for mean percent tree cover in urban parks, 2.4 percent for mean percent tree cover in residential areas, and 1.0 percent for mean percent tree cover in commercial/industrial areas. Based on these results, for our study we chose to decrease within-plot variation by increasing the size of sampling plots rather than decrease between-plot variation by increasing the number of sampling plots. The SJBE watershed is covered with 11 standard-sized FIA hexagons. Therefore, we intensified the base grid (decomposed it into smaller hexagons) by a factor of 12. We had 108 sampling points within the watershed boundaries once we removed points that fell onto census water (streams, sloughs, estuaries, canals, and other moving bodies of water at least 200 m wide, and lakes, reservoirs, ponds, and other permanent bodies of water at least 1.8 ha in area). Preliminary classification of the points using a 1991 land cover map from Helmer and others (2002) produced from LandSat Thematic Mapper imagery indicated that there are

potentially 21 points with forest, 60 urban/barren points, and 28 points on agricultural land (primarily pasture). This point distribution within the strata exceeded the minimum of 10 points per stratum for urban areas recommended by Nowak and others (2001).

Field Plot Designs

Field crews first visited the plots from July 2001 to February 2002 (hereafter referred to as the 2001 data), and then again from May 2010 to March 2011 (hereafter referred to as the 2011 data). Two plot designs were used, each with the same total sampled area 0.067 ha ($^1/_6$ acre). This plot size and number of plots gave a potential total sampled area of 7.35 ha, although the final sampled area depended on whether we had access to the sampling point.

A standard FIA subplot cluster was installed in areas that met the Caribbean FIA criteria for forested land: a contiguous area >0.4 ha, or >30 m wide for forested strips, with >10 percent canopy coverage in trees (Bechtold and Scott 2005, U.S. Department of Agriculture Forest Service 2007). In 2011, additional urban forest inventory data were collected on the FIA-style plots following FIA urban forest inventory protocols (U.S. Department of Agriculture Forest Service 2006). Single 14.6-m-radius circular plots used to collect data are part of the Urban Forest Effects (UFORE) model and thus urban forest inventories were installed in urban and agricultural lands that did not meet minimum requirements for forest under FIA's definitions (Nowak and others 2005). Small patches (>0.4 ha) of tree-covered land that did not meet the minimum area requirements were considered urbanized and usually categorized as vacant.

All plots are considered permanent and fully monumented to allow future remeasurement and assessment of forest and land use changes. Plot center is located on the ground by using Global Positioning System (GPS) units, road maps, and aerial photographs, and relocated by using previous measurements to buildings, trees, and other nearby features. When a plot center fell on a building or other surface where the center point could not be accessed, a GPS unit was used to calculate the offset location. Photographs were taken of most plot centers at both measurement periods.

[1] Nowak, D.J.; Crane, D.E.; Steven, J.C. 2002. [Untitled]. [Unpaged]. Unpublished data. On file with: Northern Research Station, Forest Inventory and Analysis, Syracuse, NY 13210.

Urban forest inventory field crews described land use and measured vegetation at systematically selected points across the San Juan Bay Estuary watershed. (photo by Jeffery Glogiewicz, Consultores Ambiental and the Fundación Puertorriqueña de Conservación)

A modified UFORE plot design was used in some areas with extremely high stem densities that still did not meet the FIA minimum size requirements for forest. These dense stands of small (diameter at breast height [d.b.h.] <12.5 cm) trees were a problem because the UFORE plot design does not subsample saplings, unlike the FIA plot design. Numbers of small trees to be measured could reach into the hundreds in these situations. In those cases tree, shrub, and ground cover estimates (described below) were made for the entire plot area, but tree measurements were taken on only one-fourth (northeast quadrant between 0 and 90 degrees) or one-half (between 0 and 180 degrees) of the plot. There was one plot in 2001 where a ¼-UFORE plot was used. In 2011 there were three plots where a ¼-UFORE plot was installed and one instance of installing a ½-UFORE plot.

Land Use, Cover, and Building Information

At each plot crews noted the land use or forest type. Developed land uses were commercial/industrial, institutional, park, residential, transportation, and vacant. The commercial/industrial land use was typified by the presence of buildings dedicated to business activities, manufacturing, etc., and included outdoor storage/staging areas as well as parking lots in downtown areas that are not connected with any institutional or residential use. Examples of a typical institutional land use would be schools, grounds of a large government agency, hospitals/medical complexes, colleges, religious buildings, and government buildings. Residential areas had buildings that were predominantly single-family or multifamily structures and their related

7

green spaces. Roads; median strips; limited access roadways; railroad stations, tracks, and yards; shipyards; airports; etc.; and their related green spaces were considered transportation land uses. Vacant areas had no apparent use, few or boarded-up buildings, and vacant structures in the immediate vicinity; were not being actively used or developed; and were not large enough or did not have enough tree cover to be considered forest. Undeveloped, nonforest land uses were agriculture (cropland, pasture, orchards, vineyards, nurseries, farmsteads, and related buildings, feed lots, and rangeland) and noncensus water bodies and wetlands (wide streams, rivers, lakes, and other water bodies). The two broadly defined forest types encountered in the SJBE watershed were mangrove forest and moist secondary forest.

At each plot the percentages of tree and shrub canopies covering the plot were estimated by visualizing the cover in a cylinder bounded by the plot boundaries and projecting it onto the ground. Trees (woody vegetation that was at least 2.5 cm d.b.h.) and shrubs (<2.5 cm d.b.h.) had to be at least 30 cm tall to be included in the estimate.

Crews estimated ground cover as a percentage of the plot area covered by buildings, impervious surfaces (for example, concrete or asphalt), permeable surfaces (such as gravel, bare soil, sand, mulch, or leaf litter), herbaceous vegetation (agricultural crops, grass, low shrubs <30 cm tall), and water. Additionally, an estimate was made of the proportion of the plot area that was available for planting trees. Cover amounts were estimated to the nearest 5 percent.

Tree and Shrub Information

The term "tree" here applies to individual woody plants that are capable of growing to a minimum d.b.h. of 12.5 cm and 5-m height. This category included palms but not nonwoody vegetation such as bananas or bamboo. Distinguishing between a tree and a shrub was often difficult and subjective. For each tree within the plot (regardless of the plot layout), distance and azimuth from plot center to the tree were noted, as were tree status (live, dead, or removed) and whether the tree falls on public lands (for example, Federal, State, or municipality). Crews also noted whether the tree is a street tree, typically meaning it was planted in the space between the edge of the road and the sidewalk; however, other examples may include areas where no sidewalks are present or median strips. A reconcile code (such as ingrowth, through growth, missed live, or missed dead) was added for plot remeasurement and every effort was made to account for all trees previously measured.

Urban forest inventory field crew assessing the condition of street trees planted along the Avenida Isla Verde, San Juan.

Tree species was noted and d.b.h. was measured at 1.4 m. For forked trees with multiple possible d.b.h. measurements, we followed the FIA guidelines described in the FIA field manuals (U.S. Department of Agriculture Forest Service 2011). Multistemmed trees such as Dypsis species palms, Ficus species, and other hedges >1.8 m tall with multiple stems >2.5 cm were treated as multiple individuals as per FIA guidelines. Height to top of tree and height to base of live crown were measured. Type, severity, and location of damage, if present, were recorded (as per the guidelines in U.S. Department of Agriculture Forest Service 2006).

Tree crown condition was evaluated by using the following parameters (see Schomaker and others 2007 for details on crown data collection protocols). Uncompacted live crown

ratio is a percentage determined by dividing the live crown length by the actual tree height. Crown light exposure describes how many sides of the tree crown receive direct sunlight. Crown density is the amount of crown branches, foliage, and reproductive structures that blocks light visibility through the crown and serves as an indicator of expected growth in the near future. Crown dieback is a percentage of the live crown area, including the dieback area. Foliage transparency is the amount of skylight visible through the live, normally foliated portion (where foliage, normal or damaged, or remnants of its recent presence can be seen) of the crown. Crown width is described with two measurements: one at the crown's widest diameter and the second at 90 degrees to the widest diameter.

For trees >6 m tall and within 18 m of buildings, distance and azimuth to the buildings were recorded to estimate the tree's impacts on building energy. Buildings were defined as space-conditioned residential structures (heated and cooled) that are ≤3 stories (2 stories + attic) in height above ground level. The UFORE model utilizes an algorithm for single standing structures ≤370 m² in total inhabitable space, although larger single-family homes or duplexes should be included regardless of size. Unheated garages, sheds, and similar outbuildings are not included.

Statistical Procedures and the Urban Forest Effects Models

Individual plot and tree data were compiled and processed by using the Urban Forest Effects (currently known as i-Tree Eco) suite of models (UFORE ACE[2] ver. 6.5). The UFORE models use data collected in the field along with hourly air pollution and meteorological data from other sources to quantify urban forest structure and function (Nowak and Crane 2000). The total number of trees and C stored in the forests and urban areas in the SJBE watershed were estimated by multiplying the estimated area in each stratum by the per-hectare estimate of each parameter calculated from the plot data. For instance, where a ¼- or ½-UFORE plot was installed, the individual tree's expansion factors were adjusted accordingly. Totals, averages, and standard errors were calculated for species, land uses, and watershed totals.

Individual tree aboveground biomass and C were estimated by using allometric equations published in scientific literature and described in Nowak (1994) and Nowak and others (2002). When multiple allometric equations existed for a single species, those equations were combined, or "splined" into a single equation (Nowak and Crane 2002).

The distance and direction of trees to adjacent buildings were measured to model the effects of tree shading on energy use.

---

[2] ACE = Anatomy, Carbon, Energy; formerly the old nomenclature for the different submodels in UFORE, now referred to as Eco.

Native and introduced trees growing on the grounds of a site that was formerly used for a governmental institution and is now classified as vacant land.

When a species-specific equation was not available, the results from using other equations for species of the same genus were averaged, and if there were no equations for the genus, then the average result from all broadleaf or conifer species equations was used (Nowak and Crane 2002). Belowground biomass and C were estimated by using an aboveground-to-belowground biomass ratio of 0.26 derived from Cairns and others (1997). Biomass values were converted to C by multiplying by 0.5 as per Nabuurs and others (2003). Leaf area and leaf biomass were estimated by using regression equations for temperate deciduous urban species described in Nowak (1996). Gross and net C sequestration were calculated according to the methods described in Escobedo and others (2010) and Nowak and others (2002, 2008).

Species richness (the number of species sampled within the watershed or each land use type) and diversity indices (Shannon-Wiener, Menhinick's, Simpson's, Shannon-Wiener evenness, and Sander's Rarefaction) for the watershed and land uses were calculated.

The reduction of energy use and the associated C emissions from power plants were estimated by using the methods described in McPherson and Simpson (1999). These savings are presented as megawatt-hours (MWh) saved that would be otherwise used for cooling residential structures, and the mega British Thermal Units and MWh that would have been used for heating.

Results

Inventory Plot Distribution

Urban forest inventory plots were installed on 99 of the 108 potential sampling points during the 2001–02 measurement period, and 94 points were relocated and measured during 2010–11 (table 1). Some potential sampling points were inaccessible, so no plots were established at either time, for example, in flooded wetland areas that were far from any roads. We categorized these areas by using aerial photographs. Other points were not sampled after landowners denied access during one or both time periods. In 2011, six sampling points were inaccessible because they were in flooded wetlands or in a mangrove forest far from any roads. Five sampling points fell in water, and access was denied by the landowner at three sampling points. Agricultural land in the Loíza area of the watershed is underrepresented by the field sampling because of a combination of impassable seasonally flooded pasture and our inability to contact landowners to gain access.

Pasture that is periodically inundated is a widespread land use in the eastern portion of the San Juan Bay Estuary watershed in the Loiza municipality. (photo by Jeffery Glogiewicz, Consultores Ambiental and the Fundación Puertorriqueña de Conservación)

Table 1—Number of plots and trees sampled by land use, area, plots sampled, number of trees, and sampled area, San Juan Bay Estuary watershed, 2001 and 2011

Land use	Area	Total area	Plots sampled		Trees		Sampled area	
			2001	2011	2001	2011	2001	2011
	- ha -	- percent -	- - - - - - - - number - - - - - - - -				- - - - ha - - - -	
Commercial/industrial/transportation	4 459	20.6	21	23	32	84	1.42	1.55
Institution/park	2 336	10.8	11	9	81	22	0.74	0.61
Mangrove forest	1 486	6.9	4	3	547	730	0.27	0.20
Residential	7 856	36.3	34	34	240	190	2.29	2.29
Moist forest	1 062	4.9	7	6	1,044	766	0.47	0.40
Vacant	3 185	14.7	15	11	86	419	1.01	0.74
Wetland/water/agriculture	1 274	5.9	7	8	NA	NA	0.47	0.54
Total	21 658	100.0	99	94	2,030	2,211	6.68	6.34

NA = not applicable.
Numbers in rows and columns may not sum to totals due to rounding.

Table 1 presents plot distribution according to primary land use categories and accessibility. Eight plots fell on wooded areas with either mangrove or moist secondary forest that was large enough to meet the FIA definition of forest, so an FIA-style subplot cluster with nested microplot was installed instead of a single, circular plot. We decided that there were too few plots in the transportation land use to analyze separately. Therefore, we grouped those plots with the commercial/industrial land. We also grouped the institutional and park categories into one category for the same reason.

From 2001 to 2011, only two sampling points changed land use category and both of these points had plots installed on them. One plot that fell on institutional land changed to vacant land after that institution's buildings were demolished and the area had yet to be redeveloped. Another area was originally categorized as vacant land recently cleared for development and had new houses on it when revisited.

Trees naturally regenerate on unused lands, in this case at the site of a closed public institution, from 2001 (left) to 2010 (right). (left photo by Jeffery Glogiewicz, Consultores Ambiental and the Fundación Puertorriqueña de Conservación; right photo by Angie Rowe, U.S. Forest Service)

Land use change from vacant, recently cleared land to a residential area (Urbanización El Coquí II) in the 10 years between urban forest inventories in the San Juan Bay Estuary watershed. (left photo by Jeffery Glogiewicz, Consultores Ambiental and the Fundación Puertorriqueña de Conservación; right photo by Edgardo González, Centro para la Conservación del Paisaje)

Land Use and Forest Cover Estimates

We estimated that mangrove and moist forests covered 2548 ha in the SJBE watershed, 11.8 percent of the area (table 1) in 2011. It should be remembered that for an area to be considered forest, it had to meet a minimum area requirement of 0.4 ha. Scattered patches of trees around the SJBE watershed were not included in the forest categories; rather they were put in the urbanized categories such as vacant/barren land use, which occupied 14.7 percent of the watershed. Residential areas were the largest single use of land in the watershed (36.3 percent), followed by urbanized areas for commercial, industrial, and transportation uses (20.6 percent) (table 1). In 2011 residential land had 24.1 percent tree cover, vacant land 22.7 percent tree cover, and land used for commercial/industrial/transportation purposes 12.2 percent tree cover (table 2). Overall, there seemed to be a pattern of increasing tree cover from 2001 to 2011 in the developed land uses, particularly in vacant land (table 2).

Tree and Shrub Canopy Cover

Field crews estimated tree and shrub canopy cover for all land uses, along with an estimate of the percentage of the plot area available for planting with additional trees or shrubs (excluding forested areas). These estimates were summarized by land use during each sampling period (table 2). There were definitional changes between the two time periods on how to estimate tree cover, shrub

Natural tree regeneration on vacant land in the San Juan Bay Estuary watershed. (photo by Jeffery Glogiewicz, Consultores Ambiental and the Fundación Puertorriqueña de Conservación)

cover, and plantable space in the forested and wetlands areas, so 2001 estimates are not comparable to the 2011 estimates. The later estimates were made with a superior procedure. Therefore, we did not include those estimates for 2001 in table 2. Estimates for the developed land uses, however, were made by using consistent procedures and are comparable.

Table 2—Mean percent tree cover, shrub cover, and plantable space with standard errors of the mean by land use, San Juan Bay Estuary watershed, 2001 and 2011

Land use	Tree cover				Shrub cover				Plantable space			
	2001		2011		2001		2011		2001		2011	
	%	SE	%	SE	%	SE	%	SE	%	SE	%	SE
Commercial/industrial/transportation	4.9	2.5	12.2	4.7	0.8	0.5	2.5	1.3	13.0	5.2	11.1	4.3
Institution/park	11.5	2.4	14.4	4.1	1.6	1.0	3.6	1.5	40.3	11.3	18.9	9.0
Mangrove forest	NA	NA	69.0	6.7	NA	NA	53.0	18.5	NA	NA	0.0	0.0
Residential	19.3	2.8	24.1	3.4	7.6	1.3	9.5	1.5	19.0	3.4	12.1	1.8
Moist forest	NA	NA	65.5	9.6	NA	NA	60.9	7.8	NA	NA	0.0	0.0
Vacant	10.0	5.0	22.7	8.3	6.1	3.2	25.9	9.8	76.9	8.6	50.0	13.4
Wetland/water/agriculture	NA	NA	0.0	0.0	NA	NA	1.3	1.3	NA	NA	12.5	12.5
Total	NA	NA	24.1	2.1	NA	NA	14.9	2.1	NA	NA	16.8	2.6

SE = standard error; NA = not applicable.

In 2011 the highest percentages of tree cover were found, of course, in the forested areas, and ranged from 65.5 to 69.0 percent (table 2, fig. 2). Residential and vacant areas had the next highest tree covers, 24.1 and 22.7 percent, respectively. Vacant areas had the highest percentage of shrub cover (25.9 percent) for developed land uses. Developed, nonvacant land uses had between 11.1 and 18.9 percent of their area available for planting additional trees or shrubs. From 2001 to 2011 there were increases in the average tree and shrub cover percentages in the developed land uses, and some indication of minor decreases in plantable space (table 2).

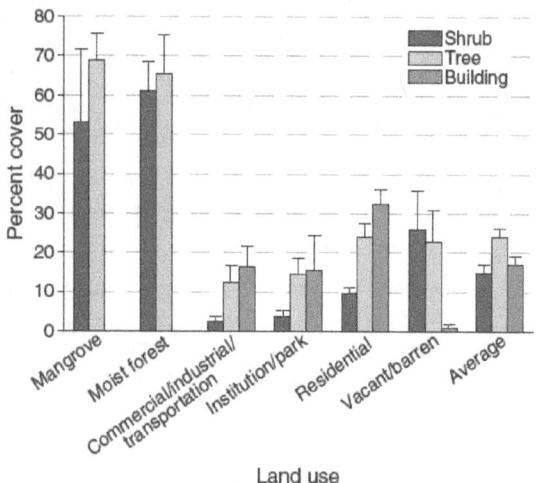

Figure 2—Percent shrub, tree and building cover by land use, San Juan Bay Estuary watershed, 2011.

Ground Cover

In table 3 we present the mean ground cover percentages by land use for 2011. The ground cover percentages for 2001 were not appreciably different from those recorded in 2011. At a typical point within the SJBE watershed, excluding larger bodies of water considered census waters, 10.6 percent of the ground was covered in duff/mulch, 20.7 percent in herbaceous plants (excluding grass), 15.9 percent in grass (both maintained and unmaintained), 8.2 percent in water, 17.0 percent with buildings, and 27.6 percent with impervious (for example, cement or tar) and other surfaces (table 3, fig. 3). For both developed land uses and undeveloped forests, on average, 55.4 percent of the ground in the SJBE watershed was covered with permeable surfaces (such as grass, vegetation, or water) and 44.6 percent was covered in impervious surfaces (such as cement, tar, or buildings).

As would be expected, forested and vacant land uses were covered almost entirely in permeable surfaces while impervious surfaces and buildings predominated in the developed land uses. Average ground cover of the two predominant urbanized land uses in the SJBE watershed, commercial and residential, is presented in figures 4 and 5.

Urban Forest Structure

Two thousand and thirty trees and shrubs from 75 species were tallied in 2001 and 2,211 trees and shrubs from 86 species were tallied in 2011. The largest trees found on the inventory plots were a mango (*Mangifera indica*) with a d.b.h. of 105 cm and a tulipán africano (*Spathodea campanulata*) with a height of 26.0 m.

As residential areas are developed and mature, the tree and shrub cover on them changes, here from 2001 (left) to 2011 (right). (photos by Jeffery Glogiewicz, Consultores Ambiental and the Fundación Puertorriqueña de Conservación)

Table 3—Mean percent ground cover with standard errors of the mean by land use, San Juan Bay Estuary watershed, 2011

Land use	Ground cover											
	Duff/ mulch		Herbaceous		Grass		Water		Building		Impervious and other	
	%	SE	%	SE	%	SE	%	SE	%	SE	%	SE
Commercial/industrial/transportation	7.0	3.0	4.3	2.4	17.5	5.6	0.0	0.0	16.4	5.3	54.8	6.9
Institution/park	3.6	2.2	3.3	1.4	43.3	13.4	1.7	1.7	15.3	9.1	32.8	9.9
Mangrove forest	28.0	17.1	17.0	8.5	0.0	0.0	55.0	24.7	0.0	0.0	0.0	0.0
Residential	6.1	1.4	9.5	2.1	16.4	3.0	0.9	0.9	32.5	3.8	34.6	3.6
Moist forest	39.4	9.3	60.6	9.3	0.0	0.0	0.0	0.0	0.0	0.0	0.0	0.0
Vacant	11.0	9.0	65.8	13.4	11.4	9.2	9.1	9.1	0.9	0.9	1.8	1.4
Wetland/water/agriculture	18.8	9.2	37.5	15.7	0.0	0.0	43.8	17.5	0.0	0.0	0.0	0.0
Total	10.6	2.1	20.7	2.5	15.9	2.5	8.2	2.4	17.0	2.0	27.6	2.2

SE = standard error.

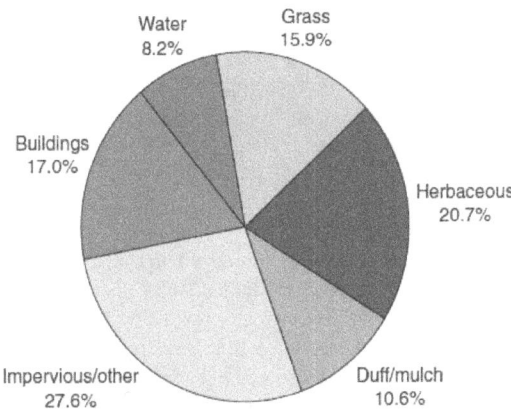

Figure 3—Average ground cover for all developed land uses combined, San Juan Bay Estuary watershed, 2011.

Revegetation of land cleared adjacent to residential developments at an urban forest inventory plot center in 2001 (top) and 2011 (bottom) in the San Juan Bay Estuary watershed. (top photo by Jeffery Glogiewicz, Consultores Ambiental and the Fundación Puertorriqueña de Conservación; bottom photo by Edgardo González. Centro para la Conservación del Paisaje)

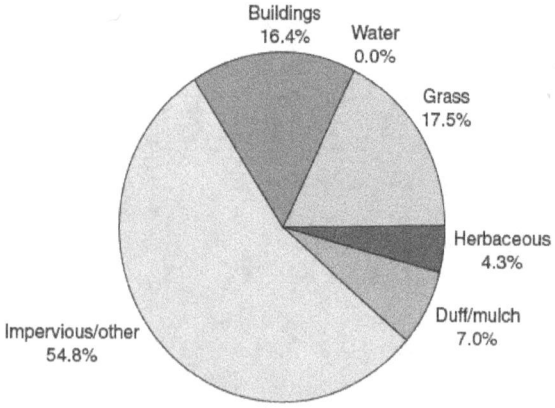

Figure 4—Average ground cover for the combined commercial/institutional/transportation land use, San Juan Bay Estuary watershed, 2011.

Patches of young, dense secondary subtropical moist forest are scattered across the San Juan Bay Estuary watershed.

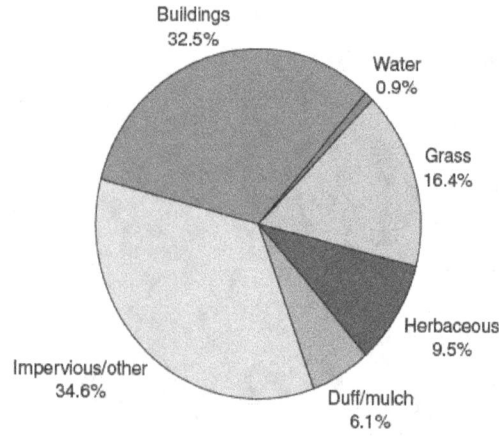

Figure 5—Average ground cover for residential land use, San Juan Bay Estuary watershed, 2011.

These sampled trees represent a total population in the watershed of 6.8 million trees (±958,000 trees) in 2001 and 10.1 million trees (±1.8 million trees) in 2011 (table 4). This tree population stored 175 255 metric tons of C in 2001 and net-sequestered 15 318 metric tons per year (table 4). The amount of C stored by the watershed's trees increased to 319 737 metric tons in 2011 and the net C sequestration rate had increased to 28 384 metric tons per year (table 4). Side-by-side comparisons of trees/ha with d.b.h. ≥2.5 cm by inventory year and land use show that mangrove and moist forest areas have much higher stem densities, C storage, and net C sequestration rates than the developed land uses, as would be expected (figs. 6, 7, and 8).

Forests have many more trees/ha but occupy less of the landscape than developed urban areas and undeveloped forests; therefore, these three land uses within the watershed store comparable amounts of total C. The 2011 estimates show that developed areas have far fewer trees (54.1 trees/ha for commercial to 564.7 trees/ha for vacant areas) and less C stored/ha (6.0 metric tons C/ha for commercial land uses to 20.3 metric tons C/ha for vacant areas) than does forest (3,607 trees/ha with 52.9 metric tons C/ha for mangroves, and 1,893 trees/ha and 43.2 metric tons C/ha for moist forest) on average (figs. 6 and 7). But there are fewer forested hectares in the watershed (2548 ha of forest, which is 11.8 percent of the total watershed land area); thus even though 72.6 percent of the trees are in mangrove and moist forests, only 38.9 percent of stored C was found there. Trees growing in urbanized areas held 61.1 percent of the stored C.

A high percentage of the trees in the SJBE watershed are of a relatively small diameter (fig. 9). The "reverse-J" distribution seen in figure 9 is commonly observed in natural forests but also typical of most urbanized landscapes. In mangrove and moist forests, 36.0 percent and 45.6 percent of tree stems were between 2.5 and 5.1 cm d.b.h. and 73.5 percent and 78.3 percent were <10.3 cm, respectively (table 5). The developed land uses had fewer saplings, ranging from a high of 63.9 percent of trees with d.b.h. <10.3 cm in vacant areas to a low of 37.4 percent in residential areas (table 5).

Table 4—Population estimates and standard error of the estimates for number of trees with d.b.h. ≥1.0 inch stored carbon, net carbon sequestration by land use for the urban forest inventory, San Juan Bay Estuary watershed, 2001 and 2011

| Land use | Number of trees | | | | Stored carbon | | | | Net carbon sequestration | | | |
| | 2001 | | 2011 | | 2001 | | 2011 | | 2001 | | 2011 | |
	- - - n - - -	- - SE - -	- - - n - - -	- - SE - -	metric tons	- - SE - -	metric tons	- - SE - -	metric tons/ year	- SE -	metric tons/ year	- SE -
Commercial/ industrial/ transportation	100,328	92,881	241,438	123,663	2 137.2	2069.9	26 585.2	14 113.5	268.9	267.9	1546.2	744.6
Institution/ park	254,390	237,875	84,656	42,453	6 433.6	5807.8	16 922.5	8 332.8	670.9	614.7	993.5	440.1
Mangrove forest	3,012,865	1,735,841	5,362,580	1,497,690	50 590.3	35 076.4	78 596.3	5 313.7	5 736.0	890.1	11 262.2	469.3
Residential	821,738	584,172	650,906	125,081	72 081.9	55 832.9	86 928.5	25 622.1	4 582.4	3 287.4	4 361.4	907.3
Moist forest	2,347,976	2,191,968	2,009,218	474,573	31 581.1	29 389.5	45 871.7	14 353.2	3 267.1	2 977.9	4 424.2	1 149.5
Vacant	271,044	232,855	1,798,653	918,495	12 429.5	11 396.1	64 833.1	34 855.6	830.3	730.7	5 796.4	2 941.4
Total	6,809,586	958,293	10,147,451	1,828,843	175 255.4	34 515.2	319 737.2	48 726.6	15 318.5	1 870.0	28 383.9	3 430.0

D.b.h. = diameter at breast height; n = number of trees; SE = standard error.

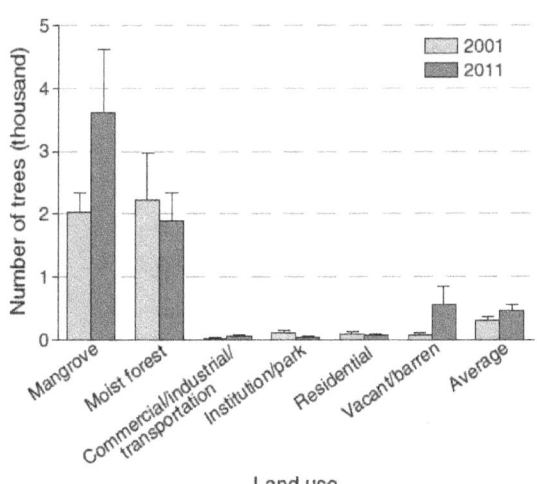

Figure 6—Number of trees/ha (with d.b.h. ≥2.5 cm) by land use, San Juan Bay Estuary watershed, 2001 and 2011.

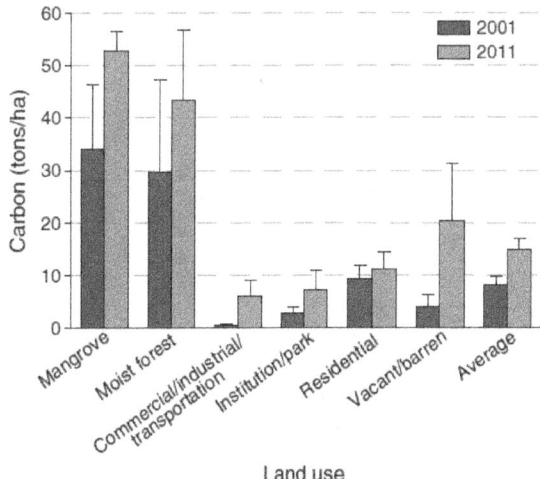

Figure 7—Carbon stored in trees/ha (with d.b.h. ≥2.5 cm) by land use, San Juan Bay Estuary watershed, 2001 and 2011.

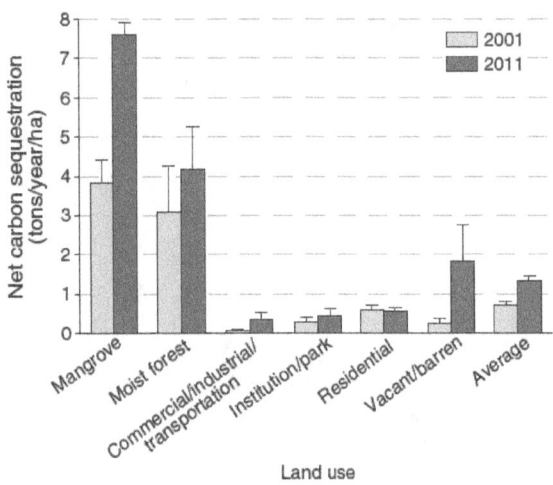

Figure 8—Net carbon annually sequestered by trees/ha (with d.b.h. ≥2.5 cm) by land use, San Juan Bay Estuary watershed, 2001 and 2011.

The author in mangrove forest in the Piñones Commonwealth Forest.

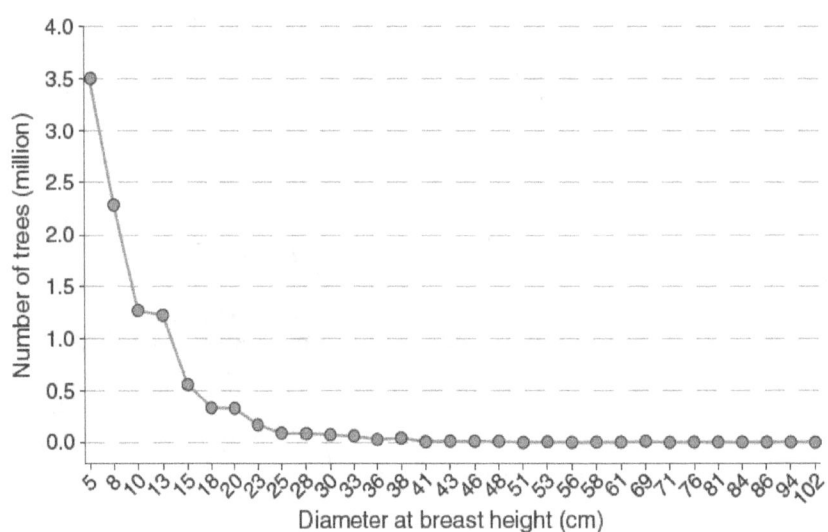

Figure 9—Number of trees (with d.b.h. ≥2.5 cm) by diameter at breast height, San Juan Bay Estuary watershed, 2011.

18

Table 5—Percentage of trees in each d.b.h. class by land use, San Juan Bay Estuary watershed, 2011

D.b.h. class	Land use						
	Commercial/ industrial/ transportation	Institution/ park	Mangrove forest	Residential	Moist forest	Vacant	Total
-- cm --				percent			
2.5–5.1	16.7	9.1	36.0	15.8	45.6	27.9	34.5
5.2–7.6	9.5	27.3	22.2	13.2	26.2	24.3	22.5
7.7–10.2	14.3	18.2	15.3	8.4	6.5	11.7	12.5
10.3–12.7	8.3	4.5	15.6	10.0	8.4	7.2	12.1
12.8–15.2	11.9	0.0	3.7	14.7	3.4	9.3	5.5
15.3–17.8	7.1	0.0	3.2	7.9	1.3	3.8	3.3
17.9–20.3	7.1	4.5	2.6	4.2	2.5	5.0	3.2
20.4–22.9	6.0	4.5	0.7	3.2	1.7	3.3	1.7
23.0–25.4	4.8	0.0	0.1	3.7	1.3	1.2	0.9
25.5–27.9	4.8	0.0	0.3	2.1	1.0	1.4	0.9
28.0–30.5	1.2	4.5	0.3	1.1	0.4	2.1	0.7
30.6–33.0	1.2	0.0	0.0	4.7	0.3	1.2	0.6
33.1–35.6	2.4	0.0	0.0	1.1	0.0	1.0	0.3
35.7–38.1	1.2	4.5	0.0	3.2	0.5	0.2	0.4
38.2–40.6	0.0	0.0	0.0	0.0	0.1	0.2	0.1
40.7–43.2	0.0	4.5	0.0	0.5	0.3	0.0	0.1
43.3–45.7	0.0	4.5	0.0	0.5	0.3	0.0	0.1
45.8–48.3	0.0	4.5	0.0	1.1	0.0	0.0	0.1
48.4–50.8	1.2	0.0	0.0	0.0	0.0	0.0	0.0
50.9–53.3	0.0	0.0	0.0	0.5	0.1	0.0	0.1
53.4–55.9	0.0	0.0	0.0	0.0	0.1	0.0	0.0
56.0–58.4	0.0	4.5	0.0	0.0	0.0	0.0	0.0
58.5–61.0	0.0	0.0	0.0	0.5	0.0	0.0	0.0
61.1–63.5	0.0	0.0	0.0	0.0	0.0	0.0	0.0
63.6–66.0	0.0	0.0	0.0	0.0	0.0	0.0	0.0
66.1–68.6	0.0	4.5	0.0	1.1	0.0	0.0	0.1
68.7–71.1	1.2	0.0	0.0	0.0	0.0	0.0	0.0
71.2–73.7	0.0	0.0	0.0	0.0	0.0	0.0	0.0
73.8–76.2	0.0	0.0	0.0	0.5	0.0	0.0	0.0
76.3–78.7	0.0	0.0	0.0	0.0	0.0	0.0	0.0
78.8–81.3	0.0	0.0	0.0	0.5	0.0	0.0	0.0
81.4–83.8	0.0	0.0	0.0	0.5	0.0	0.0	0.0
83.9–86.4	0.0	0.0	0.0	0.5	0.0	0.0	0.0
86.5–88.9	0.0	0.0	0.0	0.0	0.0	0.0	0.0
89.0–91.4	0.0	0.0	0.0	0.0	0.0	0.0	0.0
91.5–94.0	0.0	0.0	0.0	0.5	0.0	0.0	0.0
94.1–96.5	0.0	0.0	0.0	0.0	0.0	0.0	0.0
96.6–99.1	0.0	0.0	0.0	0.0	0.0	0.0	0.0
99.2–101.6	1.2	0.0	0.0	0.0	0.0	0.0	0.0

D.b.h. = diameter at breast height.
Percentages may not sum to 100 due to rounding.

Urban Forest Tree and Shrub Species Composition

Tables 6 through 12 present species composition and population estimates as well as their associated standard errors for trees with d.b.h. ≥2.5 cm, metric tons of stored C, and net annual sequestration rates for the study area and by land use. The species in these tables are ranked by total number of individuals. While this is a useful estimate, it should not be taken as the only way to assess the species' "relative importance" in the watershed. Stored C takes into account tree size, so if we were to rank species by stored carbon, a species that is less common but generally larger would rank higher than a more common species that tends to be smaller. Also, it is important to be mindful of the standard errors associated with these population estimates. In some cases our sample size was far less than ideal and this shortcoming is reflected in high sampling errors.

Our results show that red mangrove (*Rhizophora mangle*) was the most commonly encountered species overall (table 6) and in the mangrove forest (table 7). But other studies (Brandeis and others 2007, Jimenez and others 1985) have shown that the mangrove forests in the SJBE watershed have higher densities of white mangrove (*Laguncularia racemosa*) rather than red mangrove. This discrepancy can be explained by sampling methodology and sample size. One microplot (the smaller, nested plot for sampling regeneration) in our small sample of mangrove forest (three plots total in 2011) held an unusually high concentration of small red mangrove saplings. These saplings are sampled in a relatively small area so each sapling represents a large number of trees in the total population. While these mangrove forests tend toward relative overall homogeneity, it is possible that our admittedly small sample does not accurately represent the SJBE watershed's mangrove forest. We can see that the watershed's white mangrove trees store considerably more C than the red mangrove, indicating the predominance of smaller stems in the red mangrove population estimate.

The mangrove forests of the San Juan Bay Estuary watershed provide valuable ecosystem services to San Juan's population.

Moist forest showed a similar, seemingly incongruous result (table 8). With only six plots sampled in 2011, the presence of a single plot with a dense concentration of saplings can skew population estimates, particularly the estimates for total numbers of individual trees. Siamese cassia (*Senna siamea*) has the most stems in the watershed, but the tulipán africano holds the greatest amounts of stored C by far (table 8). To more accurately assess the relative importance of these species in the watershed, one should look at the total number of individuals and also their stored C, an estimate that incorporates the overall size of the trees. Note that the tulipán africano, while again not having the most individuals, also stores considerable amounts of C in the institutional/park and vacant land uses (tables 10 and 12).

Introduced species are a very important part of the SJBE watershed's forests. Tulipán africano, Siamese cassia, albizia (*Albizia procera*), flamboyán (*Delonix regia*), and guamá americano (*Pithecellobium dulce*) are all introduced species that were once purposely planted but now regenerate naturally. Flamboyán is still commonly planted for its showy flowers.

Landscapers and homeowners in the SJBE watershed preferred introduced species for planting in commercial and residential areas. Among these nonnative plants are small, ornamental palms, such as palma areca (*Dypsis lutescens*), and fruit trees such as mango, panapén (*Artocarpus altilis*), aguacate (*Persea americana*), and Citrus species. Many native moist forest species, like María, are also important parts of this urban forest community.

The showy red flowers of *Spathodea campanulata*, make it easy to see how common this introduced tree has become in the forest patches of the San Juan Bay Estuary watershed.

Table 6—Population estimates and standard error of the estimates for number of trees with d.b.h. ≥1.0 inch by common name, scientific name, number of trees measured, stored carbon, and net carbon sequestration for mangrove forest, San Juan Bay Estuary watershed, 2011

Common name	Scientific name	Number of trees			Stored carbon			Net carbon sequestration		
		%	--- n ---	-- SE --	%	metric tons	- SE -	%	metric tons/ year	- SE -
Red mangrove	*Rhizophora mangle* L.	27.5	2,791,480	1,523,408	5.8	18 582	10 144	13.9	4 020	2 015
White mangrove	*Laguncularia racemosa* (L.) C.F. Gaertn.	12.7	1,285,550	800,457	9.2	29 349	14 799	12.8	3 693	1 874
African tulip tree	*Spathodea campanulata* P. Beauv.	11.9	1,203,904	631,001	13.3	42 631	19 384	13.4	3 862	1 854
Black mangrove	*Avicennia germinans* (L.) L.	8.5	859,482	837,484	5.9	18 772	17 810	8.0	2 315	2 209
Button mangrove	*Conocarpus erectus* L.	3.5	351,967	324,051	3.6	11 653	10 090	4.7	1 358	1 207
Antilles calophyllum	*Calophyllum antillanum* Britton	3.4	345,098	255,170	2.2	6 887	4 304	2.9	823	512
Siamese cassia	*Senna siamea* (Lam.) Irwin & Barneby	3.0	304,268	301,074	0.9	2 976	2 708	1.3	376	354
Other species	—	2.5	259,796	115,281	2.2	7 293	2 942	3.1	837	294
Granadillo bobo	*Miconia prasina* (Sw.) DC.	2.3	230,824	192,785	0.2	513	351	0.7	193	144
Malabar plum	*Syzygium jambos* (L.) Alston	1.8	186,233	113,787	0.6	1 864	1 024	1.1	332	188
Citrus	*Citrus* spp.	1.6	158,771	109,014	0.6	2 074	1 297	1.3	370	227
American muskwood	*Guarea guidonia* (L.) Sleumer	1.4	142,613	137,451	0.9	2 979	2 589	1.3	371	338
Australian pine	*Casuarina equisetifolia* L.	1.4	137,367	137,351	0.8	2 653	2 652	0.8	244	244
Tall albizia	*Albizia procera* (Roxb.) Benth.	1.3	127,948	70,938	10.5	33 580	18 910	5.0	1 377	857
Gumbo limbo	*Bursera simaruba* (L.) Sarg.	1.1	107,069	82,325	1.2	3 807	2 597	1.3	372	268
Matchwood	*Schefflera morototonii* (Aubl.) Maguire, Steyerm. & Frodin	1.0	105,648	103,047	4.0	12 707	12 311	2.8	817	791
Guyanese wild coffee	*Casearia guianensis* (Aubl.) Urb.	1.0	97,051	66,809	0.1	383	256	0.4	112	71
Royal poinciana	*Delonix regia* (Bojer ex Hook.) Raf.	0.9	88,753	47,977	1.7	5 542	4 167	1.9	523	309
White cedar	*Tabebuia heterophylla* (DC.) Britton	0.8	82,819	40,437	0.9	2 931	2 016	1.2	335	185
Guamuchil	*Pithecellobium dulce* (Roxb.) Benth.	0.8	77,568	69,502	2.4	7 568	6 016	1.6	439	352
Ratwood	*Erythroxylum rotundifolium* Lunan	0.6	65,575	65,562	0.2	505	505	0.4	114	114
Punchberry	*Myrcia splendens* (Sw.) DC.	0.6	65,575	65,562	0.3	842	842	0.5	149	149
Crabwood	*Carapa guianensis* Aubl.	0.6	62,952	62,940	0.0	108	108	0.2	48	48
Spanish lime	*Melicoccus bijugatus* Jacq.	0.5	54,930	28,254	3.0	9 533	7 728	1.5	403	211
Sour orange	*Citrus ×aurantium* L. ssp. *aurantium*	0.4	41,110	23,521	0.0	150	86	0.3	85	48
Avocado	*Persea americana* Mill. var. *americana*	0.4	37,132	19,589	0.7	2 290	1 566	0.8	231	136
Cabbagebark tree	*Andira inermis* (W. Wright) Kunth ex DC.	0.3	34,815	22,301	0.8	2 471	1 668	0.6	151	93
Sapodilla	*Manilkara zapota* (L.) P. Royen	0.3	34,342	34,338	0.0	61	61	0.1	23	23
Wild honeytree	*Casearia decandra* Jacq.	0.3	34,099	34,092	0.0	85	85	0.1	33	33
Blackrodwood	*Eugenia biflora* (L.) DC.	0.3	34,099	34,092	0.0	30	30	0.1	18	18
Red stopper	*Eugenia rhombea* (Berg) Krug & Urb.	0.3	34,099	34,092	0.0	34	34	0.1	20	20
Black mampoo	*Guapira fragrans* (Dum. Cours.) Little	0.3	34,099	34,092	0.3	886	886	0.4	123	123
Geno geno	*Lonchocarpus domingensis* (Turp. ex Pers.) DC.	0.3	31,476	31,470	0.2	484	484	0.3	84	84
Bitterbush	*Picramnia pentandra* Sw.	0.3	31,476	31,470	0.0	24	24	0.1	16	16

continued

Table 6—Population estimates and standard error of the estimates for number of trees with d.b.h. ≥1.0 inch by common name, scientific name, number of trees measured, stored carbon, and net carbon sequestration for mangrove forest, San Juan Bay Estuary watershed, 2011 (continued)

Common name	Scientific name	Number of trees			Stored carbon			Net carbon sequestration		
		%	- - - n - - -	- - SE - -	%	metric tons	- SE -	%	metric tons/ year	- SE -
Bullytree	Pouteria multiflora (A. DC.) Eyma	0.3	31,476	31,470	0.0	45	45	0.1	22	22
Coconut palm	Cocos nucifera L.	0.3	30,244	16,488	0.2	796	457	0.0	10	6
Casearia	Casearia spp.	0.3	29,182	18,728	0.0	107	83	0.1	37	25
Almendra	Terminalia catappa L.	0.3	29,043	23,391	1.3	4 139	2 886	0.9	249	180
Rose	Rosa spp.	0.3	25,378	12,418	2.7	8 756	4 292	1.4	388	190
Mahogany	Swietenia macrophylla King	0.2	23,981	12,803	5.8	18 541	10 509	2.2	559	300
Portia tree	Thespesia populnea (L.) Sol. ex Corrêa	0.2	23,088	23,085	0.0	152	152	0.2	53	53
Sweet orange	Citrus ×sinensis (L.) Osbeck (pro sp.) [maxima × reticulata]	0.2	20,555	14,311	0.1	283	275	0.2	65	56
Carolina indigo	Indigofera caroliniana Mill.	0.2	19,240	19,237	0.0	72	72	0.1	34	34
Malaysian apple	Syzygium malaccense (L.) Merr. & L.M. Perry	0.2	17,171	17,169	0.2	510	510	0.2	64	64
Common guava	Psidium guajava L.	0.2	17,129	9,995	0.1	352	241	0.2	58	36
Black olive	Bucida buceras L.	0.1	14,548	10,303	1.3	4 224	3 157	0.9	264	199
Bejamin fig	Ficus benjamina L.	0.1	13,703	8,176	0.1	292	213	0.2	51	33
Guacima	Guazuma ulmifolia Lam.	0.1	13,703	13,701	0.0	78	78	0.1	34	33
Wild banyantree	Ficus citrifolia Mill.	0.1	13,395	8,519	0.2	684	456	0.3	73	46
Mango	Mangifera indica L.	0.1	13,152	6,428	2.5	7 889	5 153	1.0	265	148
Queens crapemyrtle	Lagerstroemia speciosa (L.) Pers.	0.1	11,122	8,423	4.8	15 306	11 284	1.8	469	334
Guanabana	Annona muricata L.	0.1	10,277	7,566	0.3	1 022	976	0.2	67	51
Breadfruit	Artocarpus altilis (Parkinson) Fosberg J.R. Forst. & G. Forst.	0.1	10,277	7,566	2.3	7 215	7 108	0.8	198	175
Cypress	Cupressus spp.	0.1	10,277	5,750	0.0	44	25	0.1	17	9
Yellow butterfly palm	Dypsis lutescens (H. Wendl.) Beentje & Dransf.	0.1	10,277	5,750	0.0	98	74	0.0	1	1
Broadleaf lancepod	Lonchocarpus heptaphyllus (Poir.) DC.	0.1	10,277	10,276	1.3	4 174	4 174	0.7	173	173
Barbados cherry	Muncoa pubens (A. Gray) Rollins	0.1	10,277	5,750	0.0	105	97	0.1	27	18
Queen palm	Syagrus romanzoffiana (Cham.)	0.1	10,277	10,276	0.1	226	226	0.0	3	3
Lemon bottlebrush	Callistemon pallidus (Bonpl.) DC.	0.1	8,623	8,621	0.1	422	422	0.2	51	51
River koko	Inga vera Willd.	0.1	7,869	7,867	0.2	787	787	0.2	59	59
Grapefruit	Citrus ×paradisi Macfad. (pro sp.) [maxima × sinensis]	0.1	6,852	4,770	0.1	410	288	0.2	44	31
Sea grape	Coccoloba uvifera (L.) L.	0.1	6,852	6,851	0.3	1 007	1 007	0.3	69	69
Higuillo de hija menuda	Crescentia portoricensis Britton	0.1	6,852	6,851	0.0	9	9	0.0	10	10
Barbados nut	Jatropha curcas L.	0.1	6,852	6,851	0.1	163	163	0.1	31	31
Mulberry	Morus spp.	0.1	6,852	6,851	0.1	214	214	0.1	34	34
Apamate	Tabebuia rosea (Bertol.) DC.	0.1	6,722	4,802	0.7	2 351	2 245	0.5	134	120
Clitoria	Barbieria pinnata (Pers.) Baill.	0.1	5,749	5,748	0.2	692	692	0.2	57	57
Bastard stopper	Petitia domingensis Jacq.	0.1	5,246	5,245	0.2	792	792	0.1	30	30
White pricklyash	Zanthoxylum martinicense (Lam.) DC.	0.1	5,246	5,245	0.4	1 381	1 381	0.2	67	67
Peepul tree	Ficus religiosa L.	<0.1	4,293	4,292	<0.1	32	32	<0.1	8	8

continued

23

Table 6—Population estimates and standard error of the estimates for number of trees with d.b.h. ≥1.0 inch by common name, scientific name, number of trees measured, stored carbon, and net carbon sequestration for mangrove forest, San Juan Bay Estuary watershed, 2011 (continued)

Common name	Scientific name	Number of trees			Stored carbon			Net carbon sequeseration		
		- - - n - - - -	- - SE - -	%	metric tons	- SE -	%	metric tons/ year	- SE -	
Frangipani	Plumeria rubra L.	4,293	4,292	0.0	148	148	0.1	18	18	
Areca palm	Areca spp.	3,426	3,425	<0.1	10	10	<0.1	0	0	
Ilan-ilan	Cananga odorata (Lam.) Hook. f. & Thomson	3,426	3,425	0.2	564	564	0.1	40	40	
Star apple	Chamaecrista calycioides (DC. ex Collad.) Greene	3,426	3,425	0.3	1 109	1 109	0.2	52	52	
Guara	Cupania americana L.	3,426	3,425	<0.1	16	16	<0.1	9	9	
Chinese banyan	Ficus microcarpa L. f.	3,426	3,425	<0.1	33	33	<0.1	9	9	
Tahitian gooseberry tree	Phyllanthus acidus (L.) Skeels	3,426	3,425	<0.1	6	6	<0.1	6	6	
Pumpwood	Cecropia schreberiana Miq.	2,623	2,622	0.1	474	474	0.1	29	29	
Laurel avispillo	Cinnamomum elongatum (Vahl ex Nees) Kosterm.	2,623	2,622	0.1	443	443	0.1	28	28	
Ear tree	Enterolobium cyclocarpum (Jacq.) Griseb.	2,623	2,622	<0.1	159	159	0.1	15	15	
Leadwood	Krugiodendron ferreum (Vahl) Urb.	2,623	2,622	<0.1	121	121	<0.1	13	13	
Sweetpea	Lathyrus odoratus L.	2,623	2,622	0.1	314	314	0.1	23	23	
Bastard hogberry	Margaritaria nobilis L. f.	2,623	2,622	<0.1	108	108	<0.1	12	12	
Loblolly sweetwood	Ocotea leucoxylon (Sw.) De Laness.	2,623	2,622	0.1	375	375	0.1	26	26	
Maricao	Scolosanthus portoricensis Borhidi	2,623	2,622	0.1	162	162	0.1	15	15	
Total		10,147,453	NA	99.2	319 737	NA	100.0	28 384	NA	

D.b.h. = diameter at breast height; n = number of trees measured; SE = standard error; — = no scientific name; NA - not applicable.

Percentages may not sum to 100 due to rounding.

24

Healthy, well-maintained trees in residential areas beautify and add value to properties.

Table 7—Population estimates and standard error of the estimates for number of trees with d.b.h. ≥1.0 inch by common name, scientific name, number of trees, stored carbon, and net carbon sequestraton, for mangrove forest in the urban forest inventory, San Juan Bay Estuary watershed, 2011

Common name	Scientific name	Number of trees		Stored carbon		Net carbon sequestration	
		- - - n - - -	- - SE - -	metric tons	- SE -	metric tons/ year	- SE -
Red mangrove	*Rhizophora mangle* L.	2,791,480	1,523,408	18 582	10 144	4 020	2 015
White mangrove	*Laguncularia racemosa* (L.) C.F. Gaertn.	1,285,550	800,457	29 349	14 799	3 693	1 874
Black mangrove	*Avicennia germinans* (L.) L.	859,482	837,484	18 772	17 810	2 315	2 209
Button mangrove	*Conocarpus erectus* L.	323,224	323,202	9 947	9 946	1 198	1 198
Other species	—	95,498	95,491	1 558	1 558	-4	4
Wild banyantree	*Ficus citrifolia* Mill.	7,346	7,345	388	388	40	40
Total		5,362,580	1,497,690	78 596	5314	11 262	469

D.b.h. = diameter at breast height; n = number of trees measured; SE = standard error; — = no scientific name.

Table 8—Population estimates and standard error of the estimates for number of trees with d.b.h. ≥1.0 inch stored carbon, net carbon sequestration by common name, scientific name, number of trees, stored carbon, and net carbon sequestration for moist forest in the urban forest inventory, San Juan Bay Estuary watershed, 2011

Common name	Scientific name	Number of trees		Stored carbon		Net carbon sequestration	
		- - - n - - -	- SE -	metric-tons	- SE -	metric tons/year	- SE -
Siamese cassia	*Senna siamea* (Lam.) Irwin & Barneby	304,268	301,074	2 976	2 708	376	354
African tulip tree	*Spathodea campanulata* P. Beauv.	254,431	210,183	13 334	10 915	893	755
Granadillo bobo	*Miconia prasina* (Sw.) DC.	230,824	192,785	513	351	193	144
Malabar plum	*Syzygium jambos* (L.) Alston	186,233	113,787	1 864	1 024	332	188
Citrus	*Citrus* spp.	141,642	108,332	1 892	1 286	319	223
Guyanese wild coffee	*Casearia guianensis* (Aubl.) Urb.	97,051	66,809	383	256	112	71
Antilles calophyllum	*Calophyllum antillanum* Britton	94,428	85,318	4 190	3 628	361	310
Gumbo limbo	*Bursera simaruba* (L.) Sarg.	81,313	78,193	2 424	2 198	267	247
Ratwood	*Erythroxylum rotundifolium* Lunan	65,575	65,562	505	505	114	114
Punchberry	*Myrcia splendens* (Sw.) DC.	65,575	65,562	842	842	149	149
Lancewood	*Nectandra coriacea* (Sw.) Griseb.	65,575	65,562	80	80	43	43
Crabwood	*Carapa guianensis* Aubl.	62,952	62,940	108	108	48	48
Wild honeytree	*Casearia decandra* Jacq.	34,099	34,092	85	85	33	33
Blackrodwood	*Eugenia biflora* (L.) DC.	34,099	34,092	30	30	18	18
Red stopper	*Eugenia rhombea* (Berg) Krug & Urb.	34,099	34,092	34	34	20	20
Black mampoo	*Guapira fragrans* (Dum. Cours.) Little	34,099	34,092	886	886	123	123
Geno geno	*Lonchocarpus domingensis* (Turp. ex Pers.) DC.	31,476	31,470	484	484	84	84
Bitterbush	*Picramnia pentandra* Sw.	31,476	31,470	24	24	16	16
Bullytree	*Pouteria multiflora* (A. DC.) Eyma	31,476	31,470	45	45	22	22
Cabbagebark tree	*Andira inermis* (W. Wright) Kunth ex DC.	26,230	20,583	2 426	1 667	138	92
White cedar	*Tabebuia heterophylla* (DC.) Britton	26,230	23,221	2 048	1 959	173	161
Coconut palm	*Cocos nucifera* L.	13,115	13,112	170	170	3	3
Rose	*Rosa* spp.	10,492	7,780	3 646	2 330	152	100
River koko	*Inga vera* Willd.	7,869	7,867	787	787	59	59
American muskwood	Guarea guidonia (L.) Sleumer	5,246	5,245	425	425	34	34
Pelargonium	*Pelargonium* spp.	5,246	5,245	792	792	30	30
White pricklyash	*Zanthoxylum martinicense* (Lam.) DC.	5,246	5,245	1 381	1 381	67	67
Maricao	*Scolosanthus portoricensis* Borhidi	2,623	2,622	162	162	15	15
Pumpwood	*Cecropia schreberiana* Miq.	2,623	2,622	474	474	29	29
Laurel avispillo	*Cinnamomum elongatum* (Vahl ex Nees) Koterm.	2,623	2,622	443	443	28	28
Ear tree	*Enterolobium cyclocarpum* (Jacq.) Griseb.	2,623	2,622	159	159	15	15
Wild banyantree	*Ficus citrifolia* Mill.	2,623	2,622	229	229	19	19
Other species	—	2,623	2,622	314	314	23	23
Leadwood	*Krugiodendron ferreum* (Vahl) Urb.	2,623	2,622	121	121	13	13
Bastard hogberry	*Margaritaria nobilis* L. f.	2,623	2,622	108	108	12	12
Loblolly sweetwood	*Ocotea leucoxylon* (Sw.) De Laness.	2,623	2,622	375	375	26	26
Matchwood	*Schefflera morototonii* (Aubl.) Maguire, Steyerm. & Frodin	2,623	2,622	400	400	26	26
Almendra	*Terminalia catappa* L.	2,623	2,622	711	711	37	37
Total		2,009,218	474,573	45 872	14 353	4 424	1 149

D.b.h. = diameter at breast height; n = number of trees measured; SE = standard error; — = no scientific name.

Table 9—Population estimates and standard error of the estimates for number of trees with d.b.h. ≥1.0 inch stored carbon, net carbon sequestration, and number of street trees by common name and scientific name for the commerical/industrial/transportation land use in the urban forest inventory, San Juan Bay Estuary watershed, 2011

Common name	Scientific name	Number of trees		Stored carbon		Net carbon sequestration		Street trees
		- - n - -	- SE -	metric-tons	- SE -	metric tons/ year	- SE -	- n -
Guamuchil	*Pithecellobium dulce* (Roxb.) Benth.	68,982	68,970	5 729	5 728	337	337	0
Royal poinciana	*Delonix regia* (Bojer ex Hook.) Raf.	37,365	31,872	905	751	162	135	0
Button mangrove	*Conocarpus erectus* L.	28,743	23,443	1 706	1 695	160	149	28,743
Other species	—	22,994	14,158	1 049	865	124	83	0
Almendra	*Terminalia catappa* L.	22,994	22,990	2 702	2 701	171	171	0
Tall albizia	*Albizia procera* (Roxb.) Benth.	17,246	10,361	10 985	9 599	286	204	0
Spanish lime	*Melicoccus bijugatus* Jacq.	17,246	17,243	722	722	83	83	0
Lemon bottlebrush	*Callistemon pallidus* (Bonpl.) DC.	8,623	8,621	422	422	51	51	0
Clitoria	*Barbieria pinnata* (Pers.) Baill.	5,749	5,748	692	692	57	57	0
Mango	*Mangifera indica* L.	2,874	2,874	248	248	24	24	0
Avocado	*Persea americana* Mill. var. *americana*	2,874	2,874	539	539	37	37	0
Rose	*Rosa* spp.	2,874	2,874	778	778	39	39	0
Pink trumpet-tree	*Tabebuia rosea* (Bertol.) DC.	2,874	2,874	109	109	15	15	0
Total		241,438	123,663	26 585	14 114	1 546	745	28,743

D.b.h. = diameter at breast height; n = number of trees measured; SE = standard error; — = no scientific name.

Table 10—Population estimates and standard error of the estimates for number of trees with d.b.h. ≥1.0 inch stored carbon, net carbon sequestration, and number of street trees by common name and scientific name for the institutional/park land use in the urban forest inventory, San Juan Bay Estuary watershed, 2011

Common name	Scientific name	Number of trees		Stored carbon		Net carbon sequestration		Street trees
		- - n - -	- SE -	metric tons	- SE -	metric tons/ year	SE	- - n - -
Portia tree	*Thespesia populnea* (L.) Sol. ex Corrêa	23,088	23,085	152	152	53	53	0
Carolina indigo	*Indigofera caroliniana* Mill.	19,240	19,237	72	72	34	34	0
African tulip tree	*Spathodea campanulata* P. Beauv.	15,392	15,390	6 127	6 126	316	316	0
Black olive	*Bucida buceras* L.	7,696	7,695	2 835	2 835	181	181	7,696
Queens crapemyrtle	*Lagerstroemia speciosa* (L.) Pers.	7,696	7,695	5 390	5 389	262	262	7,696
Other species	—	7,696	7,695	105	105	28	28	0
Pink trumpet-tree	*Tabebuia rosea* (Bertol.) DC.	3,848	3,847	2 242	2 242	119	119	3,848
Total		84,656	42,453	16 923	8 333	993	440	19,240

D.b.h. = diameter at breast height; n = number of trees measured; SE = standard error; — = no scientific name.

Table 11—Population estimates and standard error of the estimates for number of trees with d.b.h. ≥1.0 inch stored carbon, net carbon sequestration, and number of street trees by species for the residential land use in the urban forest inventory, San Juan Bay Estuary watershed, 2011

Common name	Scientific name	Number of trees		Stored carbon		Net carbon sequestration		Street trees
		-- n --	-- SE --	metric tons	- SE -	metric tons/ year	SE	-- n --
Other species	—	133,607	48,097	4 581	2 076	689	272	37,684
Royal poinciana	*Delonix regia* (Bojer ex Hook.) Raf.	51,387	35,861	4 637	4 099	361	278	0
Sour orange	*Citrus ×aurantium* L. ssp. aurantium	41,110	23,521	150	86	85	48	0
Spanish lime	*Melicoccus bijugatus* Jacq.	37,684	22,382	8 811	7 694	319	194	0
Avocado	*Persea americana* Mill. var. *americana*	34,258	19,377	1 752	1 470	194	131	0
White cedar	*Tabebuia heterophylla* (DC.) Britton	30,832	27,513	609	439	113	85	27,407
Mahogany	*Swietenia macrophylla* King	23,981	12,803	18 541	10 509	559	300	3,426
Tall albizia	*Albizia procera* (Roxb.) Benth.	20,555	14,311	8 441	8 221	268	237	0
Sweet orange	*Citrus ×sinensis* (L.) Osbeck (pro sp.) [maxima × reticulata]	20,555	14,311	283	275	65	56	0
Citrus	*Citrus* spp.	17,129	12,176	183	169	51	41	0
Coconut palm	*Cocos nucifera* L.	17,129	9,995	625	424	7	5	6,852
Common guava	*Psidium guajava* L.	17,129	9,995	352	241	58	36	0
Benjamin fig	*Ficus benjamina* L.	13,703	8,176	292	213	51	33	0
Guacima	*Guazuma ulmifolia* Lam.	13,703	13,701	78	78	34	33	0
Guanabana	*Annona muricata* L.	10,277	7,566	1 022	976	67	51	0
Breadfruit	*Artocarpus altilis* (Parkinson) Fosberg J.R. Forst. & G. Forst.	10,277	7,566	7 215	7 108	198	175	0
Antilles calophyllum	*Calophyllum antillanum* Britton	10,277	7,566	416	396	57	47	3,426
Cypress	*Cupressus* spp.	10,277	5,750	44	25	17	9	0
Yellow butterfly palm	*Dypsis lutescens* (H. Wendl.) Beentje & Dransf.	10,277	5,750	98	74	1	1	3,426
Broadleaf lancepod	*Lonchocarpus heptaphyllus* (Poir.) DC.	10,277	10,276	4 174	4 174	173	173	0
Barbados cherry	*Mancoa pubens* (A. Gray) Rollins	10,277	5,750	105	97	27	18	0
Mango	*Mangifera indica* L.	10,277	5,750	7 641	5 147	242	146	0
Munz's sage	*Salvia munzii* Epling	10,277	10,276	226	226	3	3	6,852
Black olive	*Bucida buceras* L.	6,852	6,851	1 389	1 389	82	82	6,852
Grapefruit	*Citrus ×paradisi* Macfad. (pro sp.) [*maxima × sinensis*]	6,852	4,770	410	288	44	31	0
Sea grape	*Coccoloba uvifera* (L.) L.	6,852	6,851	1 007	1 007	69	69	0
Barbados nut	*Jatropha curcas* L.	6,852	6,851	163	163	31	31	0
Mulberry	*Morus* spp.	6,852	6,851	214	214	34	34	0
Higuillo de hija menuda	*Crescentia portoricensis* Britton	6,852	6,851	9	9	10	10	0
African tulip tree	*Spathodea campanulata* P. Beauv.	6,852	4,770	65	61	18	14	0
Areca palm	*Areca* spp.	3,426	3,425	10	10	0	0	0
Ilan-ilan	*Cananga odorata* (Lam.) Hook. f. & Thomson	3,426	3,425	564	564	40	40	0
Casearia	*Casearia* spp.	3,426	3,425	9	9	7	7	0
Star apple	*Chamaecrista calycioides* (DC. ex Collad.) Greene	3,426	3,425	1 109	1 109	52	52	0
Guara	*Cupania americana* L.	3,426	3,425	16	16	9	9	0
Wild banyantree	*Ficus citrifolia* Mill.	3,426	3,425	66	66	14	14	0
Chinese banyan	*Ficus microcarpa* L. f.	3,426	3,425	33	33	9	9	0
Queens crapemyrtle	*Lagerstroemia speciosa* (L.) Pers.	3,426	3,425	9 916	9 915	207	207	0
Tahitian gooseberry tree	*Phyllanthus acidus* (L.) Skeels	3,426	3,425	6	6	6	6	0
Rose	*Rosa* spp.	3,426	3,425	941	941	47	47	3,426
Almendra	*Terminalia catappa* L.	3,426	3,425	726	726	41	41	0
Total		650,906	125,081	86 929	25 622	4 361	907	99,349

D.b.h. = diameter at breast height; n = number of trees measured; SE = standard error; — = no scientific name.

Table 12—Population estimates and standard error of the estimates for number of trees with d.b.h. ≥1.0 inch by common name, scientific name, number of trees, stored carbon, net carbon sequestration, and number of street trees by species for the vacant land use in the urban forest inventory, San Juan Bay Estuary watershed, 2011

Common name	Scientific name	Number of trees		Stored carbon		Net carbon sequestration		Street trees
		- - - n - - -	- - SE - -	metric tons	- SE -	metric tons/ year	- SE -	- - n - -
African tulip tree	*Spathodea campanulata* P. Beauv.	927,229	594,748	23 104	14 800	2 636	1 664	0
Antilles calophyllum	*Calophyllum antillanum* Britton	240,393	240,365	2 281	2 281	404	404	0
Australian pine	*Casuarina equisetifolia* L.	137,367	137,351	2 653	2 652	244	244	0
American muskwood	*Guarea guidonia* (L.) Sleumer	137,367	137,351	2 554	2 554	336	336	0
Matchwood	*Schefflera morototonii* (Aubl.) Maguire, Steyerm. & Frodin	103,025	103,013	12 306	12 305	790	790	0
Tall albizia	*Albizia procera* (Roxb.) Benth.	90,147	68,702	14 154	14 066	823	798	0
Sapodilla	*Manilkara zapota* (L.) P. Royen	34,342	34,338	61	61	23	23	0
Gumbo limbo	*Bursera simaruba* (L.) Sarg.	25,756	25,753	1 383	1 383	105	105	12,878
Casearia	*Casearia* spp.	25,756	18,412	98	83	29	23	0
White cedar	*Tabebuia heterophylla* (DC.) Britton	25,756	18,412	274	186	50	34	4,293
Malaysian apple	*Syzygium malaccense* (L.) Merr. & L.M. Perry	17,171	17,169	510	510	64	64	0
Cabbagebark tree	*Andira inermis* (W. Wright) Kunth ex DC.	8,585	8,584	45	45	13	13	0
Guamuchil	*Pithecellobium dulce* (Roxb.) Benth.	8,585	8,584	1 839	1 839	102	102	0
Rose	*Rosa* spp.	8,585	8,584	3 391	3 391	149	149	0
Peepul tree	*Ficus religiosa* L.	4,293	4,292	32	32	8	8	0
Frangipani	*Plumeria rubra* L.	4,293	4,292	148	148	18	18	0
Total		1,798,653	918,495	64 833	34 856	5 796	2 941	17,171

D.b.h. = diameter at breast height; n = number of trees measured; SE = standard error.

Species Diversity Indices

We sampled a slightly smaller area in 2011 (6.34 ha) compared to 2001 (6.68 ha) (table 1) but found more species overall in 2011 (86 vs. 75 species) (table 13). Residential areas were the single most species-rich land use. A diverse assemblage of native and introduced species was found there, with notable numbers of fruit trees (table 11). An increase in vacant land species richness and loss of species from the institutional/park land use in 2011 reflect the change in status of one sampling point from institutional/park to vacant land. We speculate that the increased species richness in vacant land and moist forest is due to the continued reversion of these lands to denser, more diverse forest vegetation.

Table 13 presents different species diversity indices for each land use with trees in the SJBE watershed. The Shannon-Wiener diversity index, which assumes that all species within land use type or city have been sampled, is an indicator of species richness and has a moderate sensitivity to sample size; therefore, values may not be comparable across land uses or cities.

The residential areas in the San Juan Bay Estuary watershed hold a wide variety of trees and shrubs, such as this patio in Barrio Obrero, San Juan. (photo by Jeffery Glogiewicz, Consultores Ambiental and the Fundación Puertorriqueña de Conservación)

Table 13—Tree species richness, number of species per hectare, Shannon-Wiener diversity index, Menhinick's diversity index, Simpson's diversity index, Shannon-Wiener's evenness index, and Sanders' Rarefaction technique value, San Juan Bay Estuary watershed, 2001 and 2011

Land use	Species richness		Number of species/ha		Shannon-Wiener		Menhinick		Simpson		Evenness		Rarefaction	
	2001	2011	2001	2011	2001	2011	2001	2011	2001	2011	2001	2011	2001	2011
Commercial/industrial/ transportation	9	13	6.35	8.38	1.8807	2.1439	1.5910	1.4184	5.9048	7.1288	0.8560	0.8359	7.87	7.55
Institution/park	16	7	21.56	11.53	2.2816	1.7955	1.7778	1.4924	6.5988	6.7941	0.8229	0.9227	9.79	6.53
Mangrove forest	5	6	18.53	29.65	1.2316	1.2257	0.2138	0.2221	3.0656	2.7996	0.7653	0.6841	3.82	3.84
Residential	41	41	17.88	18.31	3.1934	3.2242	2.6465	3.0470	18.2095	16.3079	0.8599	0.8626	13.64	11.45
Moist forest	32	38	67.78	93.90	2.4428	2.8763	0.9904	1.3730	6.6416	12.9478	0.7048	0.7907	9.71	10.01
Vacant	11	16	10.87	21.56	1.9318	1.7250	1.1862	0.7817	5.8762	3.3272	0.8056	0.6222	7.18	5.89
Total	75	86	11.23	13.72	3.1007	3.2766	1.6646	1.8502	11.9471	14.0792	0.7182	0.7337	NA	NA

NA = not applicable.
Note that the total watershed value for species richness will not necessarily equal the sum of the land use species richness values.

Menhinick's and Simpson's diversity indices, which are indicators of species richness and dominance, respectively, have a low sensitivity to sample size and therefore may be more appropriate for comparison between land use types. Shannon-Wiener's evenness index, which again assumes that all species within land use type or city have been sampled, is an indicator of species evenness and has a moderate sensitivity to sample size; thus, values may not be comparable across land uses or cities. Finally, Sander's Rarefaction technique value is the number of species one would expect to find if 21 trees were sampled in the land use type. For the watershed, this value is the number of species one would expect to find if 250 trees were sampled within the city.

Urban Tree Damage and Crown Health

Despite differences in damage assessment protocols from 2001 to 2011, there did not appear to be appreciable changes in the types or frequencies of pests, pathogens, or human damage agents. Individual tree damage assessments indicated that 12.7 percent of all trees in the SJBE watershed with d.b.h. ≥12.5 cm were damaged or suffered from pathogens. Damage frequency was lower in the mangrove and moist secondary forest than in developed land uses. Only 5.6 percent of mangroves showed any damage, that is, the presence of fungal fruiting bodies or advanced decay. Only 2.9 percent of moist secondary forest trees were damaged; loss of apical dominance caused by a dead terminal leader was the most common damage type. Overall, 20.3 percent of trees in developed land uses showed at least one urban damage agent, 9.1 percent had two damage agents, and 3.0 percent had three. The presence of wounds

or cracks in the bole was most common (10.3 percent), followed by cankers or decay (9.5 percent), and having the tree crown in conflict with overhead wires (8.5 percent) (table 14).

No appreciable amounts of crown dieback or defoliation were observed on the trees in the watershed during either time period, nor did there appear to be changes in tree crown conditions over time. Average crown density and foliage transparency for the most commonly encountered broadleaf trees in the watershed (with a minimum of 10 individuals) are presented in table 15 to provide a baseline for future forest health monitoring. Future decreases in crown density and foliage transparency would indicate a loss of tree vigor.

The roots of urban trees can conflict with sidewalks if they are not given sufficient growing space.

Table 14—Percentage of trees in developed land uses affected by urban damaging agents, San Juan Bay Estuary watershed, 2011

Damage agent	Percent
Wound or crack	10.3
Canker or decay	9.5
Conflict with tree crown	8.5
Severe topping or poor pruning	7.9
Vines in crown	6.2
Conflict with roots	4.6
Improper planting	0.6
Chlorotic, necrotic	0.6
Borers/bark beetles	0.6
Bark inclusion	0.6
Stem girdling	0.4
Defoliation	0.2
Excessive mulch	0.0
Dead top	0.0
Dead or dying crown	0.0

Urban Forest Effects Model Results for Ecosystem Services

The number, size, and distribution of trees in the SJBE watershed affect the functions or benefits that accrue to the local environment. An important benefit is the sequestration of C. As trees grow, they sequester or store C from the atmosphere within their biomass, thereby reducing the amount of carbon dioxide (CO_2) in the atmosphere. As CO_2 is thought by many to contribute to global climate change, reductions in this greenhouse gas through tree growth can help mitigate climate changes.

As previously mentioned, the trees in the SJBE in 2011 stored approximately 319 737 metric tons of C and sequester 28 384 metric tons of C per year (table 6). Given an estimated marginal social cost of CO_2 emissions of

Table 15—Mean crown attributes and standard errors for the estimates for the most commonly encountered broadleaf trees by common name, scientific name, number, crown ratio, crown density, and foliage transparency, San Juan Bay Estuary watershed, 2011

Common name	Scientific name	Number	Crown ratio		Crown density		Foliage transparency	
		n	mean	SE	mean	SE	mean	SE
African tulip tree	*Spathodea campanulata* P. Beauv.	99	32.0	1.6	38.4	1.4	43.6	0.6
Black mangrove	*Laguncularia racemosa* (L.) C.F. Gaertn.	49	30.9	2.5	44.2	2.8	52.1	1.6
White mangrove	*Avicennia germinans* (L.) L.	37	42.0	2.7	61.1	1.0	30.8	2.7
Red mangrove	*Rhizophora mangle* L.	35	50.4	2.9	64.0	3.7	35.0	1.6
Coconut palm	*Cocos nucifera* L.	33	53.1	4.3	59.5	1.4	42.9	0.9
Australian pine	*Casuarina equisetifolia* L.	32	88.6	1.7	28.3	0.9	59.8	0.2
Antilles calophyllum	*Calophyllum antillanum* Britton	31	39.3	3.8	39.1	3.3	41.9	1.6
Flametree	*Delonix regia* (Bojer ex Hook.) Raf.	28	55.0	3.6	29.6	2.3	46.6	2.7
Guamuchil	*Pithecellobium dulce* (Roxb.) Benth.	26	52.1	4.2	25.6	2.2	47.3	1.2
White cedar	*Tabebuia heterophylla* (DC.) Britton	25	57.8	4.1	50.0	3.0	39.0	1.4
Tall albizia	*Albizia procera* (Roxb.) Benth.	19	58.8	4.6	35.0	3.3	48.2	2.4
Button mangrove	*Conocarpus erectus* L.	19	60.0	5.5	37.5	4.6	41.0	5.4
Spanish lime	*Melicoccus bijugatus* Jacq.	17	72.1	3.8	38.8	2.2	40.6	1.7
Gumbo limbo	*Bursera simaruba* (L.) Sarg.	14	38.6	4.4	37.5	5.0	41.2	2.4
Fiddlewood	*Citharexylum spinosum* L.	13	36.9	5.0	38.3	6.0	45.0	1.4
Malaysian apple	*Syzygium jambos* (L.) Alston	13	40.4	4.5	48.6	5.7	47.9	4.3
Sour orange	*Citrus ×aurantium* L. ssp. aurantium	12	50.0	6.2	27.1	2.3	47.9	1.1
Siamese cassia	*Senna siamea* (Lam.) Irwin & Barneby	12	22.7	2.5	65.0	15.0	37.5	2.5
Avocado	*Persea americana* Mill.	11	72.3	2.9	39.1	3.1	46.4	2.0
American muskwood	*Guarea guidonia* (L.) Sleumer	10	66.0	5.3	40.0	6.8	46.5	1.7
Almendra	*Terminalia catappa* L.	10	68.5	7.2	40.0	3.9	41.5	1.7

N = number of trees measured; SE = standard error.

Table 16—Avoided energy use mega British thermal units and megawatt-hours due to the heating and cooling effects of residential houses by urban trees, with standard errors for each estimate, San Juan Bay Estuary watershed, 2011

Land use	Heating (MBtus avoided)						Heating (MWhs avoided)						Cooling (MWhs avoided)			
	Shade		Windbreak		Climate		Shade		Windbreak		Climate		Shade		Climate	
	MBtu	SE	MBtu	SE	MBtu	SE	MWh	SE	MWh	SE	MWh	SE	MWh	SE	MWh	SE
Commercial/industrial/transportation	-24,467	23,410	12,305	11,312	2,268	1,885	-1,051	1,005	530	487	95	79	3,160	3,029	1,914	1,786
Institution/park	-335	334	1,625	1,624	2,684	1,988	-14	14	70	70	112	83	14	10	403	327
Residential	-30,728	10,787	15,828	6,953	23,439	12,540	-1,320	463	682	300	979	524	8,695	2,937	4,849	1,747
Total	-55,530	25,777	29,758	13,377	28,390	12,836	-2,385	1,107	1,282	576	1,186	537	11,869	4,219	7,165	2,520

MBtu = mega British thermal units; MWh = megawatt-hours; SE = standard error.

$10.26/metric ton of C (based on the price of a ton of CO_2 trading on global markets on the http://www.pointcarbon.com/ Web site, accessed in March 2013), the estimated value of the C storage by trees in the SJBE watershed was $3.3 million with an annual C sequestration value of $291,219 in 2011, up from the 2001 values of $1.8 million in stored C and an annual rate of $157,167.

In 2011, approximately 19,034 MWh of energy required for cooling buildings were avoided due to appropriately located tree shading and climate effects in residential and commercial areas (table 16). These energy savings translate into 1 986 metric tons of avoided C emissions per year or $20,376 in economic benefits (table 17). Assuming that the price per kilowatt-hour of electricity is $0.26, an average price for the San Juan area in 2012, the energy savings from shade and climate amelioration alone equate to $4,948,840 in benefits to residents in 2011.

Table 17—Avoided tons of carbon (C) emissions due to the heating and cooling effects of residential houses by urban trees with standard errors for each estimate, San Juan Bay Estuary watershed, 2011

Land use	Heating (metric tons C avoided)						Cooling (metric tons C avoided)			
	Shade		Windbreak		Climate		Shade		Climate	
	metric tons	SE	metric tons	SE	metric tons	SE	metric tons	SE	metric tons	SE
Commercial/industrial/transportation	-538	515	271	249	49	41	321	308	194	182
Institution/park	-7	7	36	36	58	43	1	1	41	33
Residential	-676	237	348	153	511	273	884	298	493	178
Total	-1,221	567	655	295	618	280	1,206	429	728	256

C = carbon; SE = standard error.

Discussion

Urban Forest Land and Tree Cover

Ramos González and others (2005) (as cited in Lugo and others 2011) analyzed 1999 IKONOS satellite images and estimated that forest covered 26 percent of the greater San Juan metropolitan area. It is difficult to compare this estimate to the 11.8 percent forest reported in this study because in addition to the SJBE watershed, the Ramos González and others (2005) study area included more of the surrounding San Juan metropolitan area, particularly to the south with the more forested Central Cordillera foothills, and excluded the Piñones Commonwealth Forest. The spatial distribution of forest in the San Juan area is important to note, even if not explicitly addressed in this study. Tree cover is not spread equally over the watershed; rather most is concentrated in mangrove forests of the Loíza municipality, in and around the Piñones Commonwealth Forest. Outside of the concentration of mangrove located in Piñones and fringing the estuary's waterways, forest is found in scattered subtropical moist secondary forest remnants. These remnant patches are more concentrated in the upper reaches of the watershed or scattered across the area on mogote outcroppings that are too large and steep to be economically feasible for development. While the SJBE watershed's vacant areas held substantial numbers of trees, it is best to consider this forest cover as relatively ephemeral and likely to be cleared in the future.

Average U.S. urban area tree cover is 27.1 percent (Nowak and others 2001), comparable to the tree cover percentage observed in the residential and vacant land uses in the SJBE watershed, but somewhat higher than observed in the other developed land uses there. Perhaps more comparable are the results from urban areas in Florida. Using UFORE methodology very similar to that used in San Juan, Zhao and others (2010) found the city of Gainesville, FL to have 51 percent tree canopy cover, and the Miami-Dade, FL metropolitan area to have 14 percent tree canopy cover. Both of these urban areas had forested patches within the urbanized matrix: remnant oak-pine forest in Gainesville and mangrove forest in Miami-Dade.

Urban Forest Structure

To put the urban forests of the SJBE watershed into the larger context of the urban forest ecosystem, we can compare their structural characteristics to those of other urban forests. The average number of trees/ha compiled in a study of several U.S. cities ranged from 62 to 276 (Nowak and others 2001). For the SJBE watershed, the overall average tree density was 314 trees/ha, with a high of 2,211 in moist forest and a low of 22 in the commercial/institutional/transportation land use. Perhaps more comparably, Gainesville, FL, had 374 trees/ha and Miami-Dade, FL, had an average of 227 trees/ha (Escobedo and others 2010). These urban forest trees stored an average of 9.3 metric tons of C/ha in Gainesville and 38.4 metric tons of C/ha in Miami-Dade (Escobedo and others 2010). Similar to the situation in San Juan, remnant forests within the urbanized matrix and vacant land uses (2.1 metric tons/ha/year) showed the highest per-area sequestration rates in Gainesville, while Miami-Dade's mangrove forests were found to have the highest C storage density (74.7 metric tons/ha) and to be sequestering the most C per area (2.2 metric tons/ha/year) (Escobedo and others 2010).

This comprehensive forest inventory of the SJBE watershed also provides a new perspective from which to view other, more detailed, smaller-scale studies of forests in the San Juan urban landscape, and shows another dimension of the highly diverse, and heavily disturbed, subtropical moist forest of Puerto Rico. Lugo and others (2001) found an average tree density of 300 stems/ha (ranging from 22 to 879 stems/ha) for trees with a d.b.h. ≥2.5 cm in the riparian forest along the Río Piedras in the SJBE watershed. These values fall within this study's averages for forested land and urbanized areas. The riparian zones studied in Lugo and others (2001) represent heavily disturbed, less dense secondary forest found along accessible waterways in the heart of the watershed. Despiau-Batista (1997) inventoried a moist forest woodlot adjacent to the University of Puerto Rico's Botanical Garden, also in Río Piedras, and found an average of 1,701 stems/ha ≥4.0 cm d.b.h. for the 15 dominant tree species. These stem densities are comparable to those observed in this study over the entire

watershed. Plots installed along an elevational gradient on the forested mogotes that form the Bosque San Patricio Urban Commonwealth Forest found stem densities that ranged from 510 to 3,568 trees/ha and basal areas from 0.6 to 3.0 m²/ha (Suárez and others 2005).

Other studies also indicate that the urban forest of the SJBE watershed falls within the wide range of structural characteristics currently found in Puerto Rican subtropical moist forests. A stem density of 4,500 stems/ha was observed in abandoned pastures and coffee shade in the karst region (Rivera and Aide 1998). Also working in the karst region, Alvarez-Ruiz (1997) found 520 to 7,970 stems with d.b.h. ≥2.5 cm in subtropical moist forest stands at various successional stages and with varied land use histories. Chinea's (2002) study of abandoned agricultural land that had reverted to moist forest in the Humacao area found tree densities that ranged from a per-hectare low of 500 stems with d.b.h. ≥2.5 cm on very young sites to a high of 2,600 stems/ha on sites that were 43 to 45 years old (Chinea 2002).

Scattered secondary subtropical moist forest patches store and annually sequester considerable amounts of carbon every year in the San Juan Bay Estuary watershed.

Species Composition

Species composition, richness, and diversity of the two forest types found in the SJBE watershed were typical of those found in similar areas island-wide (Brandeis and others 2007). But there were also some notable differences. A striking change in species frequency occurred in the SJBE watershed's mangrove forest. The numbers of red mangrove seem to have increased considerably, but this high concentration was driven by saplings and seedlings that appeared on a single plot and has a large amount of uncertainty ascribed to it. This plot falls on a small, low-elevation island in one of the watershed's bays where debris has been cleared from the bay's side channels to increase water flow. This cleanup is part of larger efforts to rehabilitate the area since the first plot measurement. These activities might be causing changes in seawater flow around this island such that the more saltwater-tolerant red mangrove is now favored over the white mangrove, which makes up most of that small island's forest overstory. However, the standard errors associated with both of these species show these estimates overlap considerably, with standard errors >50 percent of their density estimates. Therefore, we do not see this shift in species composition as a widespread phenomenon in the watershed, but rather as a small-scale event. A similar circumstance arose with the moist forest data. Siamese cassia, while not rare, is not a ubiquitous tree in the island's subtropical moist forest. This species was found in a high concentration on one of the SJBE watershed's forested plots, inflating its total numbers, but again, the estimate is highly uncertain with a standard error >90 percent of its density estimate. These two examples highlight the sensitivity of these data to small sample sizes.

Introduced species have not become established in mangrove forests of the SJBE watershed; all species found in this forest type were native to Puerto Rico. However, outside the mangrove forests, the introduced tulipán africano is the most frequently encountered species and the species with the highest total C storage. The prevalence of tulipán africano in the SJBE watershed's forest is notable, and consistent with findings from Despiau-Batista's (1997)

study of a Río Piedras woodlot where tulipán africano was the most important (as defined by a calculated importance value) species found there. Tulipán africano and albizia were also predominant in the Bosque San Patricio when surveyed by Suárez and others (2005). Island-wide forest inventories also found that tulipán africano was the most frequently encountered species and had the highest total basal area in the island-wide forest inventories of 1990 (Franco and others 1997) and 2003 (Brandeis and others 2007). This species has steadily increased due to colonization of new areas and continued growth of established trees since the first forest inventory in 1980 (Birdsey and Weaver 1982, Brandeis and others 2007, Franco and others 1997). Some evidence suggests that tulipán africano becomes established and grows particularly well on more fertile soils on less steep slopes (Brandeis and others 2009).

Other introduced species, such as Siamese cassia and albizia, may be indicators of more intensely disturbed land within the SJBE watershed. Albizia occurred in areas which generally showed a high degree of disturbance while still allowing for some natural tree regeneration. Chinea (2002) found that albizia was more common on abandoned agricultural land that had been bulldozed, and hypothesized that the species had a competitive advantage on these heavily disturbed sites. Lugo and others (2001) reported that albizia had the highest importance value in Río Piedras riparian zones, which are also heavily affected by human activity.

Species compositions in the developed land uses differed greatly and consisted of a mix of purposely planted trees and shrubs and natural regeneration by both native and introduced species in the unmaintained areas. The high level of species richness observed in residential areas was not surprising, even when taking into account the larger number of plots sampled in that land use. Species diversity was highest in residential areas in the Miami-Dade urban forest inventory as well (Zhao and others 2010). During data collection we observed a wide variety of both native and introduced species being planted and naturally regenerating in residential areas. Tropical plant species from around the world are being used as ornamentals in San Juan and more

are being introduced, often without consideration of their potential environmental impact (for example, potential as invasive species or vectors for pests and diseases). Vacant areas were particularly diverse and dynamic. These small treed areas are undergoing primary or secondary succession depending on the time since they were last cleared or disturbed. The changing nature of the urban tree species composition in vacant areas illustrates how difficult it is to hypothesize about changes in species richness, species diversity, and persistence of introduced species and to then assess the risk from potentially invasive ones. Puerto Rico's forests are a highly diverse mix of native and introduced species that are novel assemblages, and these assemblages are still evolving (Brandeis and others 2009, Lugo and Brandeis 2005).

Note the removal of street trees that were present at the first plot measurement in 2001 (top) and their replacement with small palms when revisited in 2010 (bottom). (top photo by Jeffery Glogiewicz, Consultores Ambiental and the Fundación Puertorriqueña de Conservación; bottom photo by Edgardo González, Centro para la Conservación del Paisaje)

Tree Damage and Forest Health

These first two inventories of the watershed provided the baseline data needed to assess any future changes in tree and forest health. Although an appreciable number (12.7 percent) of the watershed's trees showed signs of natural or anthropogenic damage, there were no indications of widespread vigor declines, pests, or pathogens. Surprisingly little crown damage or dieback had occurred, for perhaps two reasons. First, past hurricanes and post-hurricane maintenance activities likely resulted in the removal of dead limbs and trees in poor condition. Sufficient time has passed since Hurricane Georges in 1998; most trees have regrown broken branches and crowns to such an extent that the damage is no longer very noticeable. The second possible reason for not recording more tree damage is the damage guidelines themselves. Our procedures may be oriented more toward recent, obvious tree damage and were not sensitive or detailed enough to record past damages. Future tree health monitoring, and unfortunately the passage of damaging hurricanes through the watershed, will provide the information needed for the assessment of our protocols.

Ecosystem Services

These initial attempts to quantify the value of the ecosystem services provided by San Juan's urban forest cover make it possible to analyze the costs and benefits related to resource management decisions. Land managers and policymakers can see that an average hectare of land (excluding the water/agriculture land use) in the SJBE watershed held 15.7 metric tons of C. For developed land uses (excluding water/agriculture, mangrove, and moist forest) the average was 10.9 metric tons of C/ha. The watershed's moist forest held an average of 43.2 metric tons/ha. This estimated C storage density is comparable to that observed in the non-urban subtropical moist forests of mainland Puerto Rico and Vieques. Using the FIA estimates for aboveground dry biomass and adding 26 percent for the belowground portion of the tree (as per UFORE calculations described in the Methods section), the forest inventory estimated C density to be 47.1 metric tons/ha in 2004 and 54.2 metric tons/ha in 2009 (Miles 2013).

Estimates for mangrove forests, however, were much more variable. We observed an average of 52.9 metric tons/ha of C. The forest inventories (using the same adjustment described above) found values of 45.5 metric tons/ha in 2004 and 25.1 metric tons/ha in 2009, but with sampling errors of 79.1 and 94.6 percent, respectively. These sampling errors produce 67-percent confidence intervals that range from a high estimate of 82.0 metric tons/ha in 2004 to a low

estimate of 1.4 metric tons/ha in 2009 (Miles 2013). The sampling intensity of mangrove forest, an important C sink in the watershed and the island as a whole, needs to be increased if we are to estimate its size accurately.

Looking farther afield, the U.S. national average urban forest C storage density is 25.1 metric tons/ha, and 53.5 metric tons/ha for all forest land (Nowak and Crane 2002). We hypothesize that the SJBE urban forest's C density values are lower than these national averages due to a combination of lower tree density in San Juan's developed land uses and smaller average tree size in the moist and mangrove forested areas.

Carbon was being sequestered at an average rate of 1.4 metric tons/ha/year across all land uses by the trees in the SJBE watershed. The highest rates of C sequestration/ha

were found in mangrove forest, where C was sequestered at a rate of 7.6 metric tons/ha/year and moist forest at 4.2 metric tons/ha/year. The average rate for developed land uses only was 0.7 metric tons/ha/year. In comparison, we can cite rates of 0.8 metric tons/ha/year for developed land uses in the continental United States (Nowak and Crane 2002) and 0.98 metric tons/ha/year in a study of urban forests in northern New England (Zheng and others 2013). The C sequestration rates observed in the SJBE watershed were near the highest values (1.7 metric tons/ha/year for urban areas in Georgia) estimated by Nowak and Crane (2002), but it should be remembered that the overall SJBE watershed rate includes a considerable area of forest, which is shown to sequester C at a higher rate than developed land uses. So it might be more accurate to compare the SJBE watershed developed land use sequestration rate of 0.7 metric tons/ha/year to U.S. urban areas.

Planted tree growth at an urban forest inventory plot center in a median strip of Paseo de los Gigantes, San Juan, from 2001 (left) to 2010 (right). (photos by Jeffery Glogiewicz, Consultores Ambiental and the Fundación Puertorriqueña de Conservación)

An illustration of rapid palm tree growth over the course of the 10-year (2001 to 2011) urban forest inventory remeasurement period at an urban forest inventory plot center in the San Juan Bay Estuary watershed. (left photo by Jeffery Glogiewicz, Consultores Ambiental and the Fundación Puertorriqueña de Conservación; right photo by Edgardo González, Centro para la Conservación del Paisaje)

In addition to the ecosystem services directly quantified in this study, trees in the SJBE watershed provided benefits that positively affected both environmental quality and human health. Closely related to the energy savings generated by urban tree shade on residential structures is the overall reduction of ambient temperature brought about by tree cover in urban areas. The formation of an urban heat island has been observed in San Juan and temperatures are thought to be increasing by 0.06 °C annually (González and others 2005, Lugo and others 2011, Velazquez-Lozada and others 2006). The SJBE watershed's urban trees will be valuable in counteracting this phenomenon, as has been shown in a meta-analysis of data collected in multiple cities, where urban green areas averaged 0.94 °C cooler than non-green sites (Bowler and others 2010).

This study did not attempt to quantify some of the most important ecosystem services trees provide in the SJBE watershed. Urban tree cover can greatly influence the flow of water through the watershed. Flooding and occasional landslides following torrential rainfall events associated with tropical depressions and hurricanes affect many San Juan residents. The prevalence of impervious surfaces in urban areas means coping with stormwater can be a problem. Tree cover reduces the impact of precipitation, stabilizes the soil, reduces rainwater runoff, and increases infiltration. The more forested Río Piedras watershed, a subwatershed within the larger SJBE watershed, has been shown to export less nitrogen than less forested urban and agricultural watersheds (Ortiz-Zayas and others 2006). In addition to reducing the amounts of nitrogen pollutants in the estuary's waters, increased forest cover could potentially help reduce the fecal coliform pollution known to be present there (Hunter and Arbona 1995).

Protection of the remaining forest cover would also help ameliorate erosion and landslides produced by poorly planned development, which are all too common throughout the upper reaches of the watershed. Natural vegetation, particularly the mangrove forest, stabilizes shorelines throughout the estuary. The economically vital San Juan Bay, through which most of the island's shipping and all of its cruise ship traffic passes, is being harmed by deteriorating water quality due to sedimentation and nutrient loads carried downstream from the surrounding urban areas (Hunter and Arbona 1995, Lugo and others 2011, Ortiz-Zayas and others 2006, U.S. Environmental Protection Agency 2007, Villanueva and others 2000). Increased tree

cover in the surrounding urban area could mitigate some of these negative human-caused environmental impacts. Selective plantings in residential and commercial areas could increase property values and provide for other recreation opportunities. Studies have shown that trees along streets and in urban lots can increase the value of properties and shorten the time it takes to sell them (Donovan and Butry 2009, Pandit and others 2013, Sander and others 2010, Saphores and Li 2012).

The delivery of all these benefits can be increased by tree-establishment programs to increase forest cover on the estimated 16.8 percent of the estuary that is potentially plantable. More efforts are needed to protect and connect urban green areas, like the consolidation of previously isolated forest patches into a more connected San Juan Ecological Corridor, which provides long-term benefits for San Juan's residents. But these benefits can also be lost by deforestation of the existing forest canopy due to poorly regulated urban development and other activities. In addition, there can be social (for example, allergies, damage to sidewalks), economic (maintenance, storm debris), and environmental (biogenic emissions, carbon emissions from decomposition) costs associated with trees (Escobedo and others 2011). Therefore, proper planning and management is needed to sustain or enhance the existing urban forest to increase the environmental and societal benefits from trees in the SJBE watershed.

Next Steps

Identifying the ecosystem services provided by subtropical urban forests that are of priority in Caribbean communities is a key point for further consideration. For example, air pollution mitigation has been identified as an important benefit of urban trees in the temperate-zone cities of the continental United States. But is it as important in a coastal city like San Juan, where regular trade winds keep air pollution concentrations low? Is the mitigation of windstorm damage by urban trees of greater value in the Caribbean?

The long-term ecological implications of the many introduced species and how they will interact with the native species as these forests grow and mature, are still uncertain. Continued inventory and monitoring efforts will help answer this and many more questions about the health and functioning of this urban forest ecosystem.

Municipal park improvements and tree planting at an urban forest inventory plot center from 2002 (top) to 2010 (bottom) in the San Juan Bay Estuary watershed. (top photo by Jeffery Glogiewicz, Consultores Ambiental and the Fundación Puertorriqueña de Conservación; bottom photo by Tom Brandeis, U.S. Forest Service)

Moreover, future ecosystem service delivery estimates for the SJBE watershed and other tropical urban areas will become more accurate as models and coefficients developed in those climates are incorporated into the UFORE/i-Tree program. For example, C sequestration was estimated in this study by using a standardized growth rate of 0.83 cm/year, which was then adjusted upward or downward according to whether the tree was in the forest or a developed land use, growing season length, crown light exposure, and tree condition (Nowak and Crane 2002). This standardized growth rate was derived from observations of trees growing in the temperate Northeast and North-Central United States. While this approach is clearly not ideal, this and other studies are now providing the information needed to adjust these growth rates for the subtropical tree species found in the SJBE watershed. Brandeis (2009) observed a mean annual growth rate of 0.37 cm/year for 2,315 trees

in the subtropical moist forest life zone on mainland Puerto Rico. Average growth rates by species were as follows: *S. campanulata*, 0.64 cm/year; *C. antillanum*, 0.41 cm/year; *A. procera*, 0.65 cm/year, with a maximum observed periodic annual increment of 2.22 cm/year; and *Pithecellobium dulce*, 1.64 cm/year (Brandeis 2009). Weaver (1979) found that trees in thinned secondary forest stands in what was then the St. Just Forest in the San Juan area grew at an average rate of 0.47 cm/year. For mangrove forest, Weaver (1979) observed that natural regeneration in cleared stands in the Piñones Commonwealth Forest grew at a rate of 0.46 cm/year from 1938 to 1975. The results from these studies and this current research will allow us to refine the models and coefficients used for future estimates of urban forest ecosystem services in San Juan and other subtropical and tropical urban areas.

Conclusions

The SJBE watershed holds species-rich, diverse forests with trees and shrubs brought there from the World's tropical regions. Despite being heavily urbanized and densely populated, the SJBE watershed maintains a relatively large, contiguous mangrove forest centered on the Piñones Commonwealth Forest that provides valuable ecosystem services to the adjoining city. In addition there are important biologically diverse secondary subtropical moist forest patches scattered across the developed urban matrix that are still in a developing stage, recovering and maturing after both recent and historical disturbances. These forests should be conserved for their ecosystem services, such as aesthetic value, recreational opportunities, and role as ecological refugia. As shown, subtropical San Juan receives considerable benefits from its diverse and vibrant urban forests.

Literature Cited

Abdollahi, K.K.; Ning, Z.H. 1996. Research update on environmental influences of trees on mitigating air pollution effects and improving urban air quality. In: Sustaining people, sustaining forests: proceedings of the 1995 Society of American Foresters national convention; October 28-November 1, 1995; Portland, ME. Bethesda, MD: Society of American Foresters: 177–185.

Alvarez-Ruiz, M.; Acevedo-Rodríguez, P.; Vázquez, M. 1997. Quantitative description of the structure and diversity of the vegetation in the limestone forest of Río Abajo, Arecibo-Utuado, Puerto Rico. Acta Científica. 11(1–3): 21–66.

Armson, D.; Stringer, P.; Ennos, A.R. 2013. The effect of street trees and amenity grass on urban surface water runoff in Manchester, U.K. Urban Forestry & Urban Greening. 12: 282–286.

Bechtold, W.A.; Scott, C.T. 2005. The forest inventory and analysis plot design. In: Bechtold, W.A.; Patterson, P.L., eds. The enhanced Forest Inventory and Analysis program—national sampling design and estimation procedures. Gen. Tech. Rep. SRS–80. Asheville, NC: U.S. Department of Agriculture Forest Service, Southern Research Station: 27–42.

Birdsey, R.A.; Weaver, P.L. 1982. The forest resources of Puerto Rico. Resour. Bull. SO–85. New Orleans: U.S. Department of Agriculture Forest Service, Southern Forest Experiment Station. 56 p.

Bowler, D.E.; Buyung-Ali, L.; Knight, T.M.; Pullin, A.S. 2010. Urban greening to cool towns and cities: a systematic review of the empirical evidence. Landscape and Urban Planning. 97: 147–155.

Brandeis, T.J. 2003. Puerto Rico's forest inventory: adapting the Forest Inventory and Analysis program to a Caribbean island. Journal of Forestry. 101(1): 8–13.

Brandeis, T.J. 2009. Diameter growth of subtropical trees in Puerto Rico. Res. Pap. SRS–47. Asheville, NC: U.S. Department of Agriculture Forest Service, Southern Research Station. 39 p.

Brandeis, T.J.; Helmer, E.H.; Marcano, H.; Lugo, A.E. 2009. Climate shapes the novel plant communities that form after deforestation in Puerto Rico and the U.S. Virgin Islands. Forest Ecology and Management. 258(7): 1704–1718.

Brandeis, T.J.; Helmer, E.H.; Oswalt, S.N. 2007. The status of Puerto Rico's forests, 2003. Resour. Bull. SRS–119. Asheville, NC: U.S. Department of Agriculture Forest Service, Southern Research Station. 75 p.

Brandeis, T.J.; Turner, J.A. 2013. Puerto Rico's Forests, 2009. Resour. Bull. SRS–191. Asheville, NC: U.S. Department of Agriculture Forest Service, Southern Research Station. 85 p.

Cairns, M.A.; Brown, S.; Helmer, E.H.; Baumgardner, G.A. 1997. Root biomass allocation in the world's upland forests. Oecologia. 111: 1–11.

Chinea, J.D. 2002. Tropical forest succession on abandoned farms in the Humacao Municipality of Eastern Puerto Rico. Forest Ecology and Management. 167: 195–207.

Departamento de Recursos Naturales y Ambientales. 2007. Inventario de flora en el corredor ecológico de San Juan, San Juan, Puerto Rico. San Juan, PR: Puerto Rico Departamento de Recursos Naturales y Ambientales, Negociado de Servicio Forestal, División de Investigación Forestal. 30 p.

Despiau-Batista, A. 1997. Distribución de las especies arbóreas de acuerdo al gradiente en topographía en el bosque de Río Piedras, Puerto Rico, luego de 60 años de abandono agrícola. Acta Científica. 11(1–3): 3–20.

Domínguez Cristóbal, C.M. 1989. La situacíon forestal pre-hispanica de Puerto Rico. Acta Científica. 3(2–3): 63–66.

Donovan, G.H.; Butry, D.T. 2009. The value of shade: estimating the effect of urban trees on summertime electricity use. Energy and Buildings. 41: 662–668.

Donovan, G.H.; Butry, D.T.; Michael, Y.L. [and others]. 2013. The relationship between trees and human health. American Journal of Preventive Medicine. 44(2): 139–145.

Escobedo, F.J.; Kroeger, T.; Wagner, J.E. 2011. Urban forests and pollution mitigation: analyzing ecosystem services and disservices. Environmental Pollution. 159: 2078–2087.

Escobedo, F.J.; Varela, S.; Zhao, M. [and others]. 2010. Analyzing the efficacy of subtropical urban forests in offsetting carbon emissions from cities. Environmental Science and Policy. 13: 362–372.

Franco, P.A.; Weaver, P.L.; Eggen-McIntosh, S. 1997. Forest resources of Puerto Rico, 1990. Resour. Bull. SRS–22. Asheville, NC: U.S. Department of Agriculture Forest Service, Southern Research Station. 45 p.

González, J.E.; Luvall, J.C.; Rickman, D. [and others]. 2005. Urban heat islands developing in coastal tropical cities. Eos, Transactions, American Geophysical Union. 86(42): 397–403..

Grau, R.H.; Hernández, M.E.; Gutierrez, J. [and others]. 2008. A peri-urban Neotropical forest transition and its consequences for environmental services. Ecology and Society. 13(1): 16. http://www.ecologyandsociety. org/vol13/iss1/art35/.

Heisler, G.M. 1986a. Effects of individual trees on the solar radiation climate of small buildings. Urban Ecology. 9: 337–359.

Heisler, G.M. 1986b. Energy savings with trees. Journal of Arboriculture. 12(5): 113–125.

Heisler, G.M.; Grant, R.H.; Grimmond, S.; Souch, C. 1995. Urban forests—Cooling our communities? In: Kollin, C.; Barratt, M., eds. Inside urban ecosystems: proceedings, 7th national urban forest conference; September 12–16; New York, NY. Washington, DC: American Forests: 31–34.

Helmer, E.H.; Ramos, O.; del Mar-López, T. [and others]. 2002. Mapping the forest type and land cover of Puerto Rico, a component of the Caribbean Biodiversity Hotspot. Caribbean Journal of Science. 38(3–4): 165–183.

Holdridge, L.R. 1967. Life zone ecology. Revised ed. San José, Costa Rica: Tropical Science Center. 206 p.

Hunter, J.M.; Arbona, S.I. 1995. Paradise lost: an introduction to the geography of water pollution in Puerto Rico. Social Science and Medicine. 40(10): 1331–1355.

Jimenez, J.A.; Martinez, R.; Encarnación, L. 1985. Massive tree mortality in a Puerto Rican mangrove forest. Caribbean Journal of Science. 21(1–2): 75–78.

Jones, R.E.; Davis, K.L.; Bradford, J. 2013. The value of trees: factors influencing homeowner support for protecting local urban trees. Environment and Behavior. 45: 650–676.

Little, E.L.; Wadsworth, F.H. 1989. Common trees of Puerto Rico and the Virgin Islands. 2nd. ed. 2 vols. Vol. 1. Washington, DC: U.S. Department of Agriculture Forest Service. 556 p.

López, T.; Aide, T.M.; Thomlinson, J.R. 2001. Urban expansion and the loss of prime agricultural lands in Puerto Rico. Ambio. 30: 49–54.

Lugo, A.E.; Brandeis, T.J. 2005. A new mix of alien and native species coexists in Puerto Rico's landscapes. Chapter 20. In: Burslem, D.F.R.P.; Pinard, M.A.; Hartley, S.E., eds. Biotic interactions in the Tropics: their role in the maintenance of species diversity. Cambridge, UK: Cambridge University Press: 484–509.

Lugo, A.E.; Ramos Gonzáles, O.M.; Rodriguez Pedraza, C. 2011. The Río Piedras watershed and its surrounding environment. Forest Ecology and Management. Rio Piedras, Puerto Rico: U.S. Department of Agriculture Forest Service, International Institute of Tropical Forestry. 48 p.

Lugo, S.; Bryan, B.; Reyes, L.; Lugo, A. 2001. Riparian vegetation of a subtropical urban river. Acta Cientifica. 15: 59–72.

Martinuzzi, S.; Gould, W.A.; Ramos González, O.M. 2007. Land development, land use, and urban sprawl in Puerto Rico: integrating remote sensing and population census data. Landscape and Urban Planning. 79: 288–297.

McCollum, J. 2001. Honeycombing the icosahedron and icosahedroning the sphere. In: Reams, G.A.; McRoberts, R.E.; Van Deusen, P.C., eds. Proceedings of the second annual Forest Inventory and Analysis symposium. Gen. Tech. Rep. SRS–47. Salt Lake City, UT: U.S. Department of Agriculture Forest Service, Southern Research Station: 25–31.

McPherson, E.G. 1994. Cooling urban heat islands with sustainable landscapes. In: Platt, R.H.; Rowntree, R.A.; Muick, P.C., eds. The ecological city: preserving and restoring urban biodiversity. Amherst, MA: The University of Massachusetts Press: 150–171.

McPherson, E.G. 1998. Atmospheric carbon dioxide reduction by Sacramento's urban forest. Journal of Arboriculture. 24(4): 215–223.

McPherson, E.G.; Rowntree, R.A. 1991. The environmental benefits of urban forests. In: A national research agenda for urban forestry in the 1990s; October; Urbana, IL. International Society of Arboriculture: 45–49.

McPherson, E.G.; Simpson, J.R. 1999. Carbon dioxide reduction through urban forestry: guidelines for professional and volunteer tree planters. Gen. Tech. Rep. PSW–171. Albany, CA: U.S. Department of Agriculture Forest Service, Pacific Southwest Research Station. 237 p.

Miles, P.D. 2013. Forest Inventory EVALIDator Web-application version 1.5.1.04. http://apps.fs.fed.us/Evalidator/tmattribute.jsp. [Date accessed: March 4].

Nabuurs, G.J.; Ravindranath, N.H.; Paustian, K. [and others]. 2003. LUCF sector good practice guidance. In: Penman, J.; Gytarsky, M.; Hiraishi, T.; Krug, T. [and others], eds. Good practice guidance for land use, land-use change, and forestry. Hayama, Kanagawa, Japan: IPCC National Greenhouse Gas Inventories Program, Technical Support Unit: 3.1–3.95. Chapter 3.

Nowak, D.J. 1993. Atmospheric carbon reduction by urban trees. Journal of Environmental Management. 37: 207–217.

Nowak, D.J. 1994. Atmospheric carbon dioxide reduction by Chicago's urban forest. In: McPherson, E.G.; Nowak, D.J.; Rowntree, R.A., eds. Chicago's urban forest ecosystem: results of the Chicago urban forest climate project. Gen. Tech. Rep. NE–186. Radnor, PA: U.S. Department of Agriculture Forest Service, Northeastern Research Station: 83-94.

Nowak, D.J. 1996. Estimating leaf area and leaf biomass of open-grown deciduous urban trees. Forest Science. 42(4): 504–507.

Nowak, D.J. 2002. The effects of urban trees on air quality. http://www. fs.fed.us/ne/syracuse/gif/trees.pdf. [Date accessed: June 2002].

Nowak, D.J.; Crane, D.E. 2000. The urban forest effects (UFORE) model: quantifying urban forest structure and functions. In: Hansen, M.; Burk, T. eds. Integrated tools for natural resources inventories in the 21st century. Proceedings of the IUFRO conference. Gen. Tech. Rep. NE–212. St. Paul, MN: U.S. Department of Agriculture Forest Service, North Central Research Station: 714–720.

Nowak, D.J.; Crane, D.E. 2002. Carbon storage and sequestration by urban trees in the USA. Environmental Pollution. 116: 381–389.

Nowak, D.J.; Crane, D.E.; Stevens, J.C.; Hoehn, R.E. 2001. The Urban Forest Effects (UFORE) model: field data collection procedures. Syracuse, NY: U.S. Department of Agriculture Forest Service, Northeastern Research Station. 51 p.

Nowak, D.J.; Crane, D.E.; Stevens, J.C. 2006. Air pollution removal by urban trees and shrubs in the United States. Urban Forestry and Urban Greening. 4: 115–123.

Nowak, D.J.; Crane, D.E.; Stevens, J.C.; Hoehn, R.E. 2005. The Urban Forest Effects (UFORE) model: field data collection manual. Syracuse, NY: U.S. Department of Agriculture Forest Service, Northern Research Station. 34 p. http://www.fs.fed.us/ne/syracuse/Tools/downloads/ UFORE_Manual.pdf. [Date accessed: January 2014].

Nowak, D.J.; Crane, D.E.; Stevens, J.C.; Ibarra, M. 2002. Brooklyn's urban forest. Gen. Tech. Rep. NE–290. Newtown Square, PA: U.S. Department of Agriculture Forest Service, Northeastern Forest Experiment Station. 107 p.

Nowak, D.J.; Dwyer, J.F.; Childs, G. 1997a. Los beneficios y costos del enverdecimiento urbano. In: Krishnamurty, L.; Rente-Nascimento, J., eds. Areas Verdes Urbanas en Latinoamérica y el Caribe. Mexico City, Mexico: Banco Interamericano de Desarrollo: 17–38.

Nowak, D.J.; Hoehn, R.E., III; Crane, D.E. [and others]. 2008. A ground-based method of assessing urban forest structure and ecosystem services. Arboriculture & Urban Forestry. 34(6): 347–358.

Nowak, D.J.; McHale, P.J.; Ibarra, M. [and others]. 1997b. Modeling the effects of urban vegetation on air pollution. In: 22nd NATO/CCMS international technical meeting on air pollution modelling and its application. Clermont-Ferrand, France. Imprimerie des UFR Sciences: 276–283.

Nowak, D.J.; Nobel, M.H.; Sisinni, S.S.; Dwyer, J.F. 2001. Assessing the U.S. urban forest resource. Journal of Forestry. 99(3): 37–42.

Ortiz-Zayas, J.R.; Cuevas, E.; Mayol-Bracero, O.L. [and others]. 2006. Urban influences on the nitrogen cycle in Puerto Rico. Biogeochemistry. 79: 109–133.

Pandit, R.; Polyakov, M.; Tapsuwan, S.; Moran, T. 2013. The effect of street trees on property value in Perth, Western Australia. Landscape and Urban Planning. 110: 134–142.

Parés-Ramos, I.K.; Gould, W.A.; Aide, T.M. 2008. Agricultural abandonment, suburban growth, and forest expansion in Puerto Rico between 1991 and 2000. Ecology and Society. 13(2): 19. http://www. ecologyandsociety.org/vol13/iss2/art1/. [Date accessed: January 2014].

Ramos González, O.M. 2001. Assessing vegetation and land cover changes in northeastern Puerto Rico: 1978–1995. Caribbean Journal of Science. 37(1–2): 95–106.

Ramos González, O.M.; Rodríguez-Pedraza, C.D.; Lugo, A.E.; Edwards, B. 2005. Distribution of forests and vegetation fragments in the San Juan metropolitan area [Abstract]. In: 9th annual urban and community forestry conference: managing the Caribbean urban and community forest, June 14–18, 2004; St. John, U.S. Virgin Islands. St. Thomas, U.S. Virgin Islands: University of the Virgin Islands, Cooperative Extension Service. 111 p.

Reams, G.A.; Smith, W.D.; Hansen, M.H. [and others]. 2005. The Forest Inventory and Analysis sampling frame. In: Bechtold, W.A.; Patterson, P.L., eds. The enhanced Forest Inventory and Analysis program— national sampling design and estimation procedures. Gen. Tech. Rep. SRS–80. Asheville, NC: U.S. Department of Agriculture Forest Service, Southern Research Station: 11–26.

Rivera, L.W.; Aide, T.M. 1998. Forest recovery in the karst region of Puerto Rico. Forest Ecology and Management. 108: 63–75.

Rowntree, R.A.; Nowak, D.J. 1991. Quantifying the role of urban forests in removing atmospheric carbon dioxide. Journal of Arboriculture. 17(10): 269–275.

Sander, H.; Polasky, S.; Haight, R.G. 2010. The value of urban tree cover: a hedonic property price model in Ramsey and Dakota Counties, Minnesota. Ecological Economics. 69: 1646–1656.

Saphores, J.D.; Li, W. 2012. Estimating the value of urban green areas: a hedonic pricing analysis of the single family housing market in Los Angeles, CA. Landscape and Urban Planning. 104: 373–387.

Schomaker, M.E.; Zarnoch, S.J.; Bechtold, W.A. [and others]. 2007. Crown-condition classification: a guide to data collection and analysis. Gen. Tech. Rep. SRS–102. Asheville, NC: U.S. Department of Agriculture Forest Service, Southern Research Station. 78 p.

Seguinot Barbosa, J. 1996. La ecología urbana de San Juan (una interpretación geográfico social). Anales de Geografía de la Universidad Complutense. 16: 161–184.

Simpson, J.R.; McPherson, E.G. 1998. Simulation of tree shade impacts on residential energy use for space conditioning in Sacramento. Atmospheric Environment. 32(1): 69–74.

Suárez, A.; Vicéns, I.; Lugo, A.E. 2005. Composición de especies y estructura del bosque kárstico de San Patricio, Guaynabo, Puerto Rico. Acta Científica. 19(1–3): 7–22.

Thompson, J.; Lugo, A.E.; Thomlinson, J.R. 2007. Land use history, hurricane disturbance, and the fate of introduced species in a subtropical wet forest in Puerto Rico. Plant Ecology. 192: 289–301.

U.S. Department of Agriculture Forest Service. 2006. Forest Inventory and Analysis national field manual. Urban inventory pilot supplement. Section 15. Urban measurements and sampling. Knoxville, TN: U.S. Department of Agriculture Forest Service, Forest Inventory and Analysis Program. 68 p. http://www.fia.fs.fed.us/library/field-guides-methods-proc/docs/core_ver_4-0_10_2007_p2.pdf. [Date accessed: June 2007].

U.S. Department of Agriculture Forest Service. 2007. Forest Inventory and Analysis national core field guide. Field data collection procedures for phase 2 plots. Version 4.0. Washington, DC 224 p. Vol. 1. Internal report. On file with: U.S. Department of Agriculture Forest Service, Forest Inventory and Analysis, 201 14th Street, Washington, DC 20250. http://www.fia.fs.fed.us/library/field-guides-methods-proc/docs/core_ver_4-0_10_2007_p2.pdf. [Date accessed: April 2007].

U.S. Department of Agriculture Forest Service. 2011. Forest Inventory and Analysis national core field guide. Field data collection procedures for phase 2 plots. Version 4.0. Washington, DC. Vol. I. Internal report. On file with: U.S. Department of Agriculture Forest Service, Forest Inventory and Analysis, 201 14th Street, Washington, DC 20250. http://www.fia.fs.fed.us/library/field-guides-methods-proc/docs/2006/core_ver_3-0_10_2005.pdf. [Date accessed: August 2011].

U.S. Environmental Protection Agency. 2007. National estuary program coastal condition report. EPA-842/B-06/001. Puerto Rico: San Juan Bay Estuary Partnership Coastal Condition. Washington, DC: U.S. Environmental Protection Agency, Office of Water, Office of Research and Development: 385–400. Chapter 7. http://water.epa.gov/type/oceb/nep/index.cfm#tabs-4. [Date accessed: January 2014].

Velazquez-Lozada, A.; Gonzalez, J.E.; Winter, A. 2006. Urban heat island effect analysis for San Juan, Puerto Rico. Atmospheric Environment. 40(9): 1731–1741.

Villanueva, E.; Rivera-Herrera, L.J.; Rivera-Colón, S. [and others]. 2000. Comprehensive conservation and management plan for the San Juan Bay Estuary. San Juan, Puerto Rico: U.S. Army Corps of Engineers. 420 p. Vol. 1.

Wadsworth, F.H. 1950. Notes on the climax forests of Puerto Rico and their destruction and conservation prior to 1900. Caribbean Forester. 11(1): 38–47.

Weaver, P.L. 1979. Tree growth in several tropical forests of Puerto Rico. Gen. Tech. Rep. SO–152. New Orleans: U.S. Department of Agriculture Forest Service, Southern Forest Experiment Station. 15 p.

Zhao, M.; Escobedo, F.J.; Staudhammer, C. 2010. Spatial pattern of a subtropical, coastal urban forest: implications for land tenure, hurricanes, and invasives. Urban Forestry and Urban Greening. 9: 205–214.

Zheng, D.; Ducey, M.J.; Heath, L.S. 2013. Assessing net carbon sequestration on urban and community forests of northern New England, USA. Urban Forestry & Urban Greening. 12(1): 61–68.

San Juan Bay Estuary. (photo courtesy of U.S. Environmental Protection Agency)

Brandeis, Thomas J.; Escobedo, Francisco J.; Staudhammer, Christina L. [and others]. 2014. San Juan Bay Estuary watershed urban forest inventory. Gen. Tech. Rep. SRS–190. Asheville, NC. U.S. Department of Agriculture Forest Service, Southern Research Station. 44 p.

We present information on the urban forests and land uses within the watershed of Puerto Rico's 21 658-ha San Juan Bay Estuary based on urban forest inventories undertaken in 2001 and 2011. We found 2548 ha of mangrove and subtropical moist secondary forests covering 11.8 percent of the total watershed area in 2011. Red, black, and white mangroves (*Rhizophora mangle*, *Avicennia germinans*, and *Laguncularia racemosa*) were the most common species due to the watershed's extensive mangrove forests, while tulipán africano (*Spathodea campanulata*) and María (*Calophyllum antillanum*) were predominant species in the moist forest patches and developed land uses. Approximately 10.1 million trees created an average tree cover of 24.1 percent, stored 319 737 metric tons of carbon (C) and sequestered C at a rate of 28 384 metric tons/year. This stored C had an estimated value of $8.1 million with an annual C sequestration value of $718,113 in 2011, up from the 2001 values. In 2011 approximately 19 000 megawatts of energy required for cooling buildings were avoided due to tree shading and climate effects in residential and commercial areas and equated to 1986 metric tons of avoided C emissions due to building energy effects.

Keywords: Caribbean, ecosystem services, FIA, forest inventory, Puerto Rico, subtropical forest, urban forest.

How do you rate this publication?
Scan this code to submit your feedback or go to
www.srs.fs.usda.gov/pubeval

www.ingramcontent.com/pod-product-compliance
Lightning Source LLC
Chambersburg PA
CBHW080612290526
45790CB00007B/2740